Army Uniforms
Since 1945

Digby Smith

Army Uniforms
Since 1945

BLANDFORD PRESS

Poole   Dorset

First published in the U.K. 1980
Copyright © 1980 Blandford Press Ltd,
Link House, West Street,
Poole, Dorset BH15 1LL

British Library Cataloguing in Publication Data
Smith, Digby
  Army uniform since 1945. – (Blandford colour series).
  1. Uniforms, Military – History – 20th century
  I. Title
  355.1'4'0904   UC480

ISBN 0 7137 0991x

Phototypeset in Monophoto Apollo
by Oliver Burridge and Co. Ltd.
Printed in Hong Kong
by South China Printing Co.

Contents

Introduction

In this book an effort has been made to show the uniforms of the armies and irregular forces engaged in actual fighting throughout the world and also the uniforms of the forces of N.A.T.O. and Warsaw Pact countries which are constantly engaged in the 'Cold War'.

Considerable detail has also been given on equipment and weapons as well as 'buttons and bows' so that a broader and deeper impression can be gained of the forces covered.

The campaign histories included are necessarily exceedingly brief but should provide a factual basis so that those who wish to research further will at least have the correct date of the operations involved and the locations over which they were conducted.

I am most grateful for the help given to me in the preparation of this book by Mike Chappell, who has provided many of the most interesting colour plates based on his own collection of references and his personal experiences serving as a professional soldier in various parts of the globe. Similarly, Martin Windrow has been very generous in allowing me to draw on his extensive library of reference material particularly in the areas of French involvement in Algeria and Indo-China.

Without their help, this book would have been much less well balanced and interesting.

Digby Smith, July 1979

The Cold War

Since 1945 there has been armed peace in Europe with the forces of East and West glaring at each other over the Iron Curtain. The West formed the military side of the North Atlantic Treaty Organisation (N.A.T.O.) on 4 April 1949 and it now includes Belgium, Canada, Holland, Luxemburg, West Germany, Denmark, Iceland, Italy, Norway, Portugal, Greece, Turkey, the United Kingdom and U.S.A.

In response to this the Warsaw Pact (WARPAC) was formed in eastern Europe in 1955 and includes Russia, East Germany, Czechoslovakia, Bulgaria, Hungary, Rumania and Poland. The Warsaw Pact has been active in earnest twice—once in 1956 to crush the Hungarian uprising and again in 1968 to suppress Czechoslovakia's bid for freedom.

Over the last six or seven years the balance of power between these groups has swung steadily in favour of the East as far as conventional weapons is concerned and the recent signing of S.A.L.T. 2 in Vienna will scarcely have affected this situation. Western experts are agreed that Russia has far more conventional forces than she needs for pure defence and despite her differences with China, the bulk of these remain firmly either in Eastern Europe or in Western Russia.

Approximate relative strengths (1978/9) are:

	N.A.T.O.	WARPAC
Armoured Divisions	14 (11,000 tanks)	38 (27,200 tanks)
Mechanized Divisions	20	57
Infantry and Airborne Divisions	30	8
Totals	64	103
Light Bombers	150	175
Fighters (ground attack)	2,125	1,675
Interceptors	600	3,050

The Malayan Emergency

During World War II the Malayan People's Anti-Japanese Army (M.P.A.J.A.) had been formed in Malaya mainly recruited from Chinese

9

ex-patriots. It was headed by Lai Teck and was an ineffective force. By the end of the war it had eight regiments with 6,000 men in all. In March 1947 Lai Teck absconded with all the Malayan Communist Party (M.C.P.) funds (the M.C.P. was the political force behind the M.P.A.J.A.) and Lau Yew took over; in February 1948 the M.P.A.J.A. became the anti British M.P.A.B.A. but strength had now dropped to 1,000. By June 1948 they had 3,000 men and operated in the rural areas intimidating peasants and attacking rubber planters and isolated police posts. The Malayan government declared a state of emergency in parts of Johore and Perak states on 16 June 1948 and one month later Lau Yew was killed by security forces near Kajang. He was replaced by Chea Ping and on 1 February 1949 the M.P.A.B.A. became the Malayan Races' Liberation Army with a strength of 4,000 men and women, mainly Chinese. The security forces soon realised that the only way to root out these terrorists (who had set up camps in the jungle where they lived in safety) was to form small, specialist teams to penetrate the jungle and use it to their advantage to track down and destroy the M.R.L.A. The other major government breakthrough was the process of removing villagers from exposed locations in the jungle and re-settling them in defended sites so that the terrorists were denied access to food, shelter and information. Chinese suspected of co-operating with terrorists were punished by being repatriated to mainland China.

Aboriginal tribesmen were recruited by the government as scouts and trackers and formed their own fighting unit, the 'Senoi Praak'.

Gradually the security forces gained the upper hand and in July 1960 the emergency was ended. Casualties during the 12-year war were:

	Killed	Wounded	Captured	Surrendered*
M.R.L.A.	6,710	—	1,287	2,702
Malayan Police	1,246	1,601	—	—
British Army	519	959	—	—
Civilians	2,473	1,385	810 (missing)	

* Terrorists who surrendered were rehabilitated and rewarded with sums of money.

The Korean War

From 1910 to 1945 Korea was occupied by Japan; at the peace negotiations in 1945 it was decided that the country would be placed under

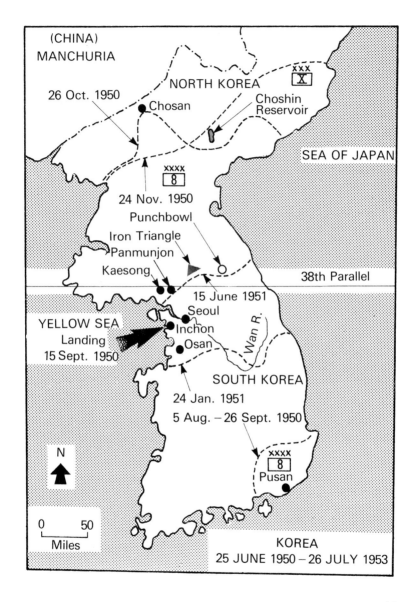

(CHINA)
MANCHURIA

NORTH KOREA

26 Oct. 1950

Chosan

Choshin Reservoir

SEA OF JAPAN

XXXX
8

24 Nov. 1950

Punchbowl
Iron Triangle
Panmunjon
Kaesong

38th Parallel

15 June 1951

Seoul

YELLOW SEA
Landing
15 Sept. 1950

Inchon

Osan

Wan R.

SOUTH KOREA

24 Jan. 1951

5 Aug. – 26 Sept. 1950

N

XXXX
8

Pusan

0   50
Miles

KOREA
25 JUNE 1950 – 26 JULY 1953

11

joint Allied administration, the South being under American control, the north (from the 38th Parallel) being under Soviet control. (Soviet Russia declared war on Japan a few weeks before the end of the war.) The United Nations (U.N.) decided that elections should be held in Korea in 1948 to form a government to take over from the allied administration. This was done in South Korea but the Soviets refused to permit the elections to take place in the north. On 15 August 1948 the Republic of Korea was proclaimed in the south with Syngman Rhee as president and this was followed on 9 September 1948 by the declaration in North Korea of a Democratic People's Republic with authority over the whole of the Korean peninsula. In December 1948 Russia assured the world that she had withdrawn all her forces from North Korea but refused to allow U.N. verification. By June 1949 all but a few U.S. troops had left South Korea—those remaining being small training advisory teams.

The balance of forces was now as follows:

	North Korea	South Korea
Army	127,000 men	98,000 men in 8 divisions
Border Guards	19,000	nil
Tanks	150	nil
Aircraft	200	nil
Ships	nil	small coastal force

Many North Koreans had served with the Chinese Communist army from 1939-45, the army was well equipped with Soviet weapons and had been trained by Soviet instructors. Four of the eight South Korean divisions were equipped with American light weapons and light artillery but they had no anti-tank weapons or heavy artillery. The other four divisions had only light infantry weapons of Japanese manufacture. On 25 June 1950 North Korea invaded the south and advanced on Seoul. In the pandemonium at UN headquarters the Soviet delegation boycotted Security Council meetings and on 27 June (in their absence) the council adopted the American resolution 'to furnish such assistance to the Republic of Korea as may be necessary to repel the armed attack'. That same day President Harry S. Truman authorized use of the U.S. Air Force and Navy and followed this on 30 June 1950 with promise of U.S. Army help. General Douglas MacArthur was appointed U.N. commander and the land forces allied with the Americans included The Commonwealth Division consisting of three infantry brigades with artillery and armour (one British brigade, one Canadian and one partly British, Australian and New Zealander); one Turkish infantry brigade; infantry elements also being drawn from Thailand, Philippines, France, Greece, Netherlands, Belgium, Luxemburg, Columbia and Ethiopia. South Africa, Denmark, Italy, Norway, Sweden and India each contributed a field ambulance team.

By 5 August 1950 a U.S. army detachment had been overrun at Osan and the U.N. forces were confined around the southern port of Pusan where the U.S. Eighth Army (Lt-Gen. W. H. Walker) conducted a successful defence.

The Korean Peninsula lends itself to amphibious warfare and the Americans made use of this; on 15 September 1950 the U.S. Navy landed the U.S. X Army Corps (Maj.-Gen. E. M. Almond) in the enemy rear at Inchon while the Eighth Army broke out of the Pusan perimeter to meet them. The North Korean army broke under these attacks and fled north. By 26 October 1950 advance elements of the Eighth Army were at the Yalu River at Chosan (the Chinese border) and the chase was stopped. The North Koreans lost 100,000 prisoners alone and were crushed as a fighting force. The pendulum swung rapidly back however when 300,000 Chinese army 'volunteers' poured into North Korea on 25 November 1950 and by the 15 December the Eighth Army was back at the 38th Parallel; X Corps was cut off but withdrew to Hungnam where it was successfully evacuated by the U.S. navy. General Walker was killed in a car crash on 23 December and General Matthew B. Ridgway took over command of the Eighth Army. By now combined R.O.K., U.S. and U.N. strength was 365,000 men but on 1 January 1951 they were attacked by half a million Chinese; three days later the Chinese occupied Seoul but the offensive died out by 24 January due to heavy U.S. air attacks on the Chinese logistic supply lines.

A U.N. counter-attack was launched on 25 January and by 23 April they had pushed the Chinese back 20 miles north of the 38th Parallel. International politics had now taken a hand and the U.S. government forbade General MacArthur to attack any targets on the far side of the Yalu River. MacArthur strongly resented this limitation of his powers and on 11 April 1951 he was sacked by President Truman and General Ridgway took over as U.N. commander. General James A. Van Fleet assumed command of the Eighth Army. A Chinese counter-offensive forced ground to be given up again and by 15 June 1951 the line had stabilised across the 38th Parallel.

On 23 June 1951 the Soviets proposed a ceasefire in Korea, this was agreed to and truce talks began at Panmunjon. They lasted for over two years before an armistice was finally achieved and much bloody fighting took place during this time, much of it in the 'Iron Triangle' and the 'Punchbowl'. The truce was finally signed on 26 July 1953 (U.S. date), 27 July (Korean date). Since then there have been repeated armed clashes along the ceasefire line and no true peace yet exists.

Casualties in this war were: Americans—33,629 killed, 103,284 wounded, 4,753 wounded and missing; Chinese—900,000 killed and wounded; North Koreans—520,000 killed and wounded; other U.N. forces (including South Koreans)—74,000 killed, 250,000 wounded, 83,000 missing and prisoners; Civilians—400,000 killed and wounded.

The Vietnam Wars

In 1946 the natives in French Indo-China (Vietnam, Laos and Cambodia) began to agitate for independence from France and this campaign soon became the First Indo-China War, a military struggle which culminated with the crushing French defeat at Dien Bien Phu where 50,000 Viet Minh guerrillas surrounded and overran 10,000 French troops in a fifty-five day battle lasting from 13 March to 7 May 1954. On 21 June of that year a cease-fire was agreed to by both sides at the Geneva conference and French Indo-China became independent. Since 1949 the four states (North and South Vietnam, Laos and Cambodia) had been quasi-independent parts of the French empire but there was considerable friction between the aggressive Vietnamese and their placid neighbours. In 1953 Viet Minh forces invaded Cambodia and in 1954 regular North Vietnamese troops repeated the violation. Following French withdrawal from the area in 1954 most of the rebel Khmer Issarak guerrillas in Cambodia had surrendered to the royalist government there and the International Control Commission (sent to the area following Geneva) was withdrawn in December 1969 at the request of Prince Sihanouk (Cambodian premier). Three months later he was deposed and on 9 October 1970 the Khmer Republic was proclaimed. It enjoyed U.S. support.

In South Vietnam a republic was proclaimed on 26 October 1955 with Madame Ngo Dinh-Diem as president and prime minister and in the Democratic Republic of North Vietnam Ho Chi Minh was president.

The Second Indo-China War began in 1957 when North Vietnamese terrorists (masquerading as South Vietnamese rebel Viet Cong) attacked

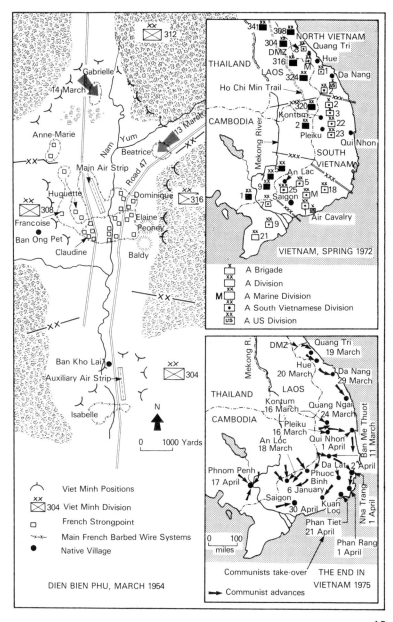

DIEN BIEN PHU, MARCH 1954

Viet Minh Positions

Viet Minh Division

French Strongpoint

Main French Barbed Wire Systems

Native Village

VIETNAM, SPRING 1972

A Brigade

A Division

A Marine Division

A South Vietnamese Division

A US Division

THE END IN VIETNAM 1975

Communists take-over

Communist advances

15

South Vietnam.

The first U.S. military advisers were sent to help South Vietnam shortly after this invasion and by November 1963 their number had risen to 16,000. In November of that year President Diem of South Vietnam was overthrown and it is thought that the U.S.A. may have helped remove him as his regime was so corrupt. In August 1964 the Gulf of Tonkin incident occurred in which it was alleged that North Vietnamese gunboats had attacked U.S. vessels. President L. B. Johnson (in office since Kennedy's assassination in November 1963) had Congress authorize the 'Gulf of Tonkin Resolution'—a formal declaration of American support for South Vietnam in the war—although subsequent investigation showed that the Resolution had been drafted by the president *before* the incident took place in the Gulf of Tonkin! U.S. involvement in the Vietnam war rose dramatically; in April 1969 over half a million U.S. servicemen were involved and as early as 1965 North Vietnam was being heavily bombed.

South Korea, Thailand, the Philippines, Australia and New Zealand also sent contingents to help the South Vietnamese but that nation was divided (the Catholic minority ruled the Bhuddist majority) and corruption was rife so that the Viet Cong rebels survived in the country-side.

North Vietnamese regular army divisions were used in this war and their logistic supply routes ran south through Laos and Cambodia to the Mekong delta and Saigon areas. Cambodia and Laos were too weak to stop these infringements.

On 30 January 1968 the North Vietnamese, judging conditions ripe for a transition from guerrilla to open warfare, launched the 'Tet Offensive' and their troops were soon fighting in the suburbs of many South Vietnamese cities including Saigon and Hué. After two weeks however their offensive was broken and their losses in dead alone are estimated at 32,000 against 1,000 Americans and 2,000 South Vietnamese.

On 31 March 1968 there was a partial halt to the heavy U.S. bombing of the north and in May that year America and North Vietnam met in Paris for peace talks. They were joined on 31 October by South Vietnamese government and communist South Vietnamese 'National Liberation Front' delegates.

By December 1970 the 'Gulf of Tonkin Resolution' scandal was uncovered, the resolution repealed and the numbers of U.S. troops in Vietnam reduced. Richard Nixon (president since January 1969) continued these reductions to 184,000 in December 1971 and by mid-1972 U.S. involvement had almost ended.

In March 1972 the Paris talks were broken off by the U.S.A. and this was followed by a renewed North Vietnamese offensive with the U.S. retaliating by mining Haiphong and six other North Vietnamese harbours. The Paris negotiations were then renewed in July 1972 but in December Henry Kissinger reported to the president that there seemed to be no chance of success whereupon the United States renewed intensive bombing of North Vietnam for eleven days. This forced North Vietnam back to the negotiating table and peace was signed on 27 January 1973. Under its terms, North Vietnam was empowered to keep her troops in South Vietnam: U.S. troops were withdrawn.

The U.S. and South Vietnam had intervened in the war in Cambodia in April and June of 1970 and the Khmer Rouge evolved as the armed communist rebel group with Chinese support. Lon Nol's Cambodian government staggered on for five years but the Khmer Rouge ousted it in 1975. They then embarked on a totally ruthless campaign of population redistribution which is estimated to have caused over 2 million civilian deaths.

In Laos the pro-Soviet Pathet Lao overthrew the government in May 1975.

The situation in South Vietnam seemed reasonably stable but in 1975 the North Vietnamese renewed their offensive in the central highlands and quite suddenly the South Vietnamese army collapsed. The whole country fell to the North Vietnamese; Saigon being captured on 30 April 1975 and shortly afterwards being renamed 'Ho Chi Minh'.

Cambodia was the next seat of war. On 25 December 1978 the United Democratic Republic of Vietnam's army, supported by 4,000 Soviet advisers and backing the 'Kampuchean National United Front for National Salvation' (K.N.U.F.N.S.) invaded Cambodia, threw out the pro-Chinese Khmer Rouge and their bestial 're-education' policies and installed a pro-Soviet People's Revolutionary Council to rule the country. Prince Sihanouk was released from house arrest in China to go to the United Nations to plead for international action to stop the Vietnamese and K.N.U.F.N.S. invasion of Cambodia but he achieved nothing. Some elements of the Khmer Rouge fled into Thailand and there is a danger that the war will spread into that country. The Vietnamese attack on Cambodia led directly to the Chinese punitive attack on Vietnam in February and March 1979.

The casualties in the Second Indo-China war are estimated at:

	Killed	Wounded
United States	46,397	306,653
South Vietnamese Armed Forces	254,257	783,602
North Vietnamese Armed Forces and Viet Cong	925,000	2 to 3 million

The China-Vietnam Clash

In 1977 the Chinese People's Liberation Army (ground forces only) consisted of $2\frac{1}{2}$ million men in 111 divisions which were organized into 37 corps. In addition there were the following independent divisions: 8 infantry, 9 armoured, 3 anti-tank, 21 artillery, 5 cavalry, 11 railway construction and 20 border guards (10 on the Mongolian and 10 on the Soviet border). The Air Force has 30 divisions with 4,000 planes and there is a very small navy of about 160,000 men (including 30,000 marines), 1,700 surface vessels and 66 submarines dedicated to a coastal patrol role. China's surface-to-surface missiles include some with ranges of up to 5,500 km. Of the army 30 divisions form the Production and Construction Corps and are employed in industrial or agricultural projects. They are armed only with light, personal weapons.

There is also a huge, semi-trained militia of about 12 million men and women only part of which is armed.

On 17 February 1979, following the Vietnamese invasion of Cambodia and the overthrow of the pro-Chinese Khmer Rouge regime there, China invaded Vietnam in a limited punitive expedition employing about 30 divisions (200,000 men in all) at Lao Cai, Cao Bang, Lang Son (Friendship Pass) and Mon Cai on the coast.

Apart from the Tibetan campaign and subsequent clashes with Khamba guerrillas and Soviet border guards, the Chinese army lacks combat experience. The Vietnamese forces however, have been almost constantly at war since 1948 and from reports of the fighting it seems that the Chinese suffered extremely heavy losses and that their battle procedures were easily and repeatedly upset by the Vietnamese operating from well-dug-in positions. Only small advances were achieved (perhaps that was all that was desired) and an exchange of prisoners is now underway following the end of the fighting in mid-March.

Apparently only the commanders' tanks down to platoon level had radios fitted; communication below this level being by means of signal flags which must make operations in poor visibility or at night extremely hazardous.

In early May 1979, the Deputy Chief of Chinese Defence Staff, General Wu Xiuquan, announced that Chinese casualties in the 17-day war were 20,000 and claimed that Vietnam had lost 50,000.

China held 1,600 Vietnamese prisoners and Vietnam claims to have captured 240 Chinese.

The Indo-Pakistani Conflicts

In 1947 India achieved independence from Britain and was at once split into two main states. The mainly Hindu and Sikh central part became India, the mainly Moslem north western and north eastern parts became Pakistan. This partition had been at the express insistence of Mohammed Ali Jinnah and other Moslem leaders who refused to attempt to continue living in a mixed religious community. Each of the many states in the old British India was to be given the choice of joining the new India or Pakistan and generally they were permitted to do as their ruling bodies voted but there were important exceptions; Jammu and Kashmir being one and Hyderabad (Sind) another. In Hyderabad the legislative assembly voted 33 to 20 to join Pakistan but the Hindu ruler decided to join India and Indian troops soon confirmed his decision; in Jammu and Kashmir (with a population 80 per cent. Moslem) the Hindu ruler decided directly to join India and the state was soon under Indian control.

Indian troops also invaded the minor state of Junagadh on 9 November 1947 and secured it for their country. Even prior to Partition, religious feelings had been running high in the sub-continent and the uprooting of 12 million people, who had to move into the new states of their choice, caused endless misery which burst into bloody conflict all too often. It is estimated that over a million civilians died in the rioting and massacres which accompanied this event.

Partition of India had brought with it a splitting up of the 'British' Indian forces with the army being divided as follows:

	to India	to Pakistan
Infantry regiments	15	8
Armoured car regiments	12	6
Artillery regiments	18.5	8.5
Engineer regiments	61	34

The old infantry regiments going to India included: 2nd Punjab Regiment, The Madras Regiment, the Grenadiers, the Mahratta Light Infantry, the Rajputana Rifles, the Rajput Regiment, the Jat Regiment, the Sikh Regiment, Dogra Regiment, the Gahrwal Rifles, The Kumaon Regiment, the Assam Rifles, the Sikh Light Infantry, the Bihar Regiment and the Mahar Regiment. Cavalry regiments included Skinner's Horse, Gardner's Horse, Hodson's Horse, King George V's Own Light Cavalry and King Edward VII's Own Light Cavalry.

Pakistan took the 1st, 8th, 14th, 15th and 16th Punjab Regiments, the Baluch Regiment, the Frontier Force Regiment and the Frontier Force Rifles while cavalry units included Probyn's Horse, the 6th and 13th Lancers, King George V's Own Lancers and Prince Albert Victor's Own Cavalry.

Students of British military history will be glad to know that the best British regimental traditions are carefully maintained in regiments of both armies of the Indian sub continent.

The declaration of Kashmir's ruler for India, and its position, lying up against Pakistan's north eastern border was too much of a provocation for Pakistan. Firstly irregular Moslem tribesmen crossed into Kashmir and attacked police posts and in October 1947 India and Pakistan were at war in the province. The conflict remained localized in the mountains and by 1 January 1949 both sides agreed to a U.N. cease-fire which left India holding two thirds of Jammu and Kashmir, Pakistan holding the northern and eastern remainder which they term Azad Kashmir (Free Kashmir), the Indian held portion being called 'Ghulam Kashmir' (Slave Kashmir).

It was recommended by the U.N. commission that India should hold a plebiscite in Kashmir and abide by the decision of the people as to which state they wished to join; this plebiscite has still not been held.

While India chose to go her own way after partition, Pakistan sought international support; in 1954 she concluded a mutual defence treaty with the U.S.A. and in the September joined S.E.A.T.O. In 1955 she joined C.E.N.T.O. but left it in 1977. On the Pakistani political scene the military soon came to power when General Mohammed Ayub Khan was appointed prime minister by president Mirza in 1958. Ayub Khan then ousted Mirza in a coup on 27 October 1958.

Due to her treaty links, Pakistan had been able to replenish her armoury with modern weapons and enjoyed qualitative superiority over her Indian rival. This was to change however in a strange manner.

China had reasserted her control over Tibet in 1950 after defeating her internal Nationalist enemies under Chiang Kai-Shek who withdrew to Formosa (Taiwan). The Tibetans accepted Chinese rule in 1951 but in 1958 a full scale revolt against the Chinese broke out in Lhasa and quickly spread all over Tibet. The Chinese crushed the revolt and the Dalai Llama (Tibet's temporal and spiritual ruler) fled to India as did several thousand Khamba tribesmen who continued to raid the Chinese occupation troops across the borders from Nepal and India for some years. To maintain her Tibetan garrisons more easily, China built a road across the Aksai Chin area of Kashmir and thus came into conflict with India who claimed the territory as theirs. There were other border disputes with India in the North East Frontier Agency (N.E.F.A.) where the 'MacMahon line' was generally recognized as the frontier.

The tension grew between India and China in these widely separated disputed areas, both extremely remote and rugged with most terrain being over 25,000 feet in height. Pandit Nehru, India's prime minister, decided to adopt a 'forward policy' on both fronts even though the Indian army was not equipped for a prolonged operation in such high, remote terrain, had very few specialist mountain troops and even these were not wholly acclimatized to the combat altitude. On top of this the Indian brigade and divisional commanders, realising the impracticality of attempting to adopt an offensive role with the limited, ill-equipped available troops advised against it.

They were ignored and hostilities broke out (in very low key) in December 1961. The Chinese enjoyed massive numerical superiority in both contested regions and their troops were well equipped and acclimatized to the high altitude as they had been fighting the Khamba rebels for years. The action was mainly limited to platoon level outpost bickering but on 9 September 1962 Indian defence minister, Krishna Menon, decided on his own initiative to order the Indian army in the N.E.F.A. to push the Chinese from Thag La ridge, just east of Bhutan, in operation Leghorn. India had twenty-five infantry battalions scattered along the N.E.F.A. and while the Chinese had three divisions, these were concentrated, two being at Tawang (behind Thag La ridge) and one at Walong at the eastern end of N.E.F.A. The 7th Indian Brigade was ordered to carry out the task but the brigade commander refused and his divisional commander supported him.

Both officers were replaced and the desired attack was put in on 20 September. Chinese response was steady but effective; they poured through Thag La pass and through Tulung pass a few miles to the east and swept the Indians down through Sela and Bomdilla to Chaku on

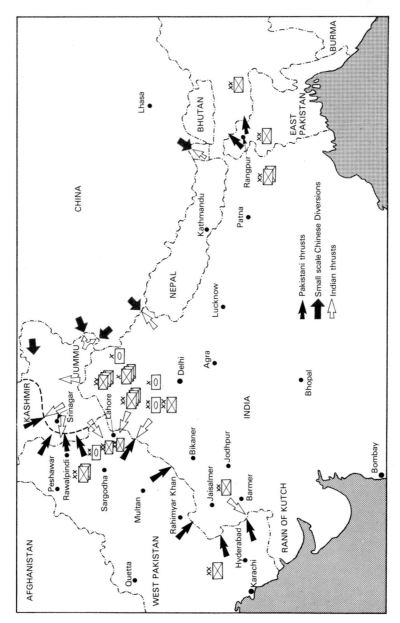

the road to Tezpur.

The defeat was complete and a ceasefire was agreed on 21 November 1962. Indian losses were 1,383 killed, 1,696 missing, 3,968 captured (90 per cent of these were in N.E.F.A., the rest in the Aksai Chin area). Chinese losses were 400 killed and an unknown number wounded. Some of the Indian regiments involved in the thick of the fighting were the Parachute Brigade, 4th Garhwal Rifles, 1st/8th Gurkhas, 1st/9th Gurkhas, Guards, 1st Sikhs, 9th Punjabis, Grenadiers and Assam Rifles.

This stinging defeat caused India to expand her army by six new mountain divisions as well as other units and Britain and U.S.A. quickly replenished her depleted arsenals with modern weapons and equipment, including the Vickers tank. Thus it came about that India's lack of modern armaments was remedied and she became a more dangerous foe for Pakistan.

The 1965 Indo-Pakistani War

There has never really been peace between these two states and border clashes have occurred periodically from 1947 on. Seeing India's growing military strength after the 1961 'war' with China, Pakistan began to woo that neighbouring giant as a counterweight to cancel out India's quantitative supremacy. By 1965 leading Pakistani generals and politicians thought it necessary to teach India a lesson by ejecting her from certain disputed areas in the Rann of Kutch—an extensive salt marsh and desert tract on the coast south east of Karachi. In April 1965 a short and effective campaign was mounted which achieved the capture of Biar Bet and Point 84 and the Pakistani army's morale rose considerably. It was however doubtful if their government had really weighed the likely reaction of India to this satisfying slap in the face.

India ordered general mobilization and Pakistan followed suit. The balance of forces was:

Divisions	India	Pakistan
Armoured	$1\frac{1}{2}$	$1\frac{1}{4}$
Mountain	9 (2 still forming)	—
Infantry	6	6 (1 in East Pakistan)
Men	825,000	230,000
Tanks	Centurions— 210	400 (M47 and M48)
	Shermans— 30	
	Stuarts— 80	
	AMX 13— 40	

| Militia and territorial army | 100,000 | 320,000 (including Azad Kashmir force, Frontier Corps, West Pakistan Rangers and East Pakistan Rifles (10,000)) |

Both armies were organized and trained on British lines.

In August 1965 about 3,000 Kashmiri 'Freedom Fighters' infiltrated into Indian-held Kashmir for sabotage purposes but most were quickly captured by the Indians. On 16 August an Indian battalion crossed the cease-fire line near Kargil in Kashmir and occupied three important mountain features; two more such attacks were mounted on 24 August at Tithwal (in West Kashmir) and another near Naushara (in south west Kashmir). The Pakistanis were active in the north west at Keran, Mirpur, Uri, Mendhar and Chamb. On 27 August an Indian brigade group attacked the 'Uri-Poonch Bulge' from the north and next day captured the Haji-Pir Pass, a traditional route for infiltrators from Pakistan.

The major actions in this war took place around Lahore, an area crossed from north east to south west by three major rivers—the Chenab, Ravi and Sutlej/Beas from north to south. It was also cut by three canals running south from the Chenab, through the Ravi and along the Sutlej—this was the Ichhoril canal—the Upper Chenab canal—lying between Chenab and Ravi—and a third canal running between and parallel to the Ravi and Sutlej/Beas. The intervening country was low lying, liable to flooding and covered in many parts by head-high sugar cane. It was thus an area unsuitable for armoured warfare.

Pakistan opened the action here on 1 September when one infantry and two armoured brigades crossed the border north of the Chenab, driving east on Chamb and brushing aside the two Indian battalions there. In the close and difficult country the advance was halted some miles short of Akhnur. The Indian response came on 6 September when five separate brigade attacks were launched towards the vulnerable Pakistani border city of Lahore on the front from Ferozepore to Amritsar.

The northernmost of these armoured supported columns was aimed at Jassar, the second from Amritsar on Lahore; the third was a few miles south and also aimed at Lahore; the fourth and fifth at Kasur. The Pakistanis had fortified the Ichhoril Canal (120 ft. wide by 15 ft. deep) and it presented a formidable tank obstacle even though only lightly-manned and the Indian advance was held along its length.

By 7 September the Pakistanis committed their armoured division in a counterattack in the Kasur area but, after bloody fighting, the assault was abandoned as it could make no headway against the Indian anti-tank defence. This action was known as the Battle of Asal Uttar. Indian efforts to breach the Ichhoril canal line were equally unsuccessful. On 8 September the Indians launched their armoured division and two infantry divisions from Jammu against Sialkot in two prongs but the hastily-reconstituted Pakistan armoured division was rushed up and stopped the advances about ten miles inside the frontier. As both tank forces outstripped their lorry-borne infantry on the rough terrain, there was a series of tank-to-tank battles lasting in all fifteen days and known as the Battle of Phillora (10-12 September) and the Battle of Chawinda (14-17 September). It seems that the British Centurion tank came out better than the American Patton due to its higher rate of fire and simpler procedures.

As soon as open warfare broke out both Britain and the U.S. had cut off supplies of arms and ammunition to both warring parties and the offensives began now to die out as stocks became exhausted. A U.N. ceasefire was agreed to on 23 September and in January 1966 Soviet premier Alexei Kosygin brought the two states together in Tashkent where they agreed to withdraw to positions held on 15 August 1965.

India claims to have gained 740 square miles of territory and Pakistan 1,600 square miles.

Casualties were declared by each side as follows:

	India	Pakistan
Killed	2,212	1,030
Wounded	7,636	2,171
Captured or missing	1,500	630

As most damaged tanks were recovered and repaired, the losses in this campaign are not known. Due to lack of movement, very few were captured.

Both air forces were used in the ground attack, reconnaissance and interdiction roles and Pakistan seems to have come out on top. Pakistan admits losing fourteen planes, India admits thirty-five.

Both sides made the mistake of using tanks in unsuitable terrain.

In March 1971 East Pakistan's Awami League leader, Mujibur Rahman, set up a provisional government independent of that in West

Pakistan. Rahman was arrested and widespread unrest broke out which was quietly supported from India. East Pakistani dissidents were trained and armed in India and formed the Mukti Bahini who then re-entered their own country and fought a guerrilla war against the West Pakistani authorities and army there. In November 1971 India invaded East Pakistan, ignoring a U.N. ceasefire call in December; by the end of the year the West Pakistani army in the new 'Bangladesh' collapsed and 60,000 were captured.

In West Pakistan Zulfikar Ali Bhutto (leader of the parliamentary majority) ousted the military leader General Agha Mohammed Yahya Khan (who had been in power since 1968) and released Mujiba Rahman who returned to Bangladesh to assume the leadership. Bhutto was overthrown by a military coup led by his chief of staff General Mohammed Zia ul-Haq on 5 July 1977 and executed in 1979.

Since August 1971 India and the U.S.S.R. have been linked by a treaty of friendship while Pakistan remains associated with China for arms supply.

In 1975 India annexed the tiny Himalayan kingdom of Sikkim, thus fuelling the fires of Pakistan's fears for her own integrity even further.

The Arab-Israeli Wars

Following World War II, with its horrific Nazi extermination of over 6 million Jews, there was a heavy exodus of surviving Jews from Europe to Palestine. Britain tried unsuccessfully to limit Jewish immigration but by mid 1947 the situation in Palestine was so explosive that she gave up trying to administer her mandate there and asked the U.N. to mediate between Jew and Arab. On 29 November 1947 the U.N. General Assembly adopted a resolution for the partition of Palestine into two states and next day fighting broke out between the Arab and Jewish communities there.

The Jewish para-military Haganah and Palmach (15,000 strong) were engaged with Palestinian Arabs aided by irregulars from neighbouring states including Syria, Lebanon, Jordan, Egypt, Iraq and Saudi Arabia. Despite these apparent odds, the Jews managed to strengthen their position by 14 May 1948 when a truce was declared and the British forces and administration left the country. Two Jewish terrorist groups also took part in the fighting—the Irgun Zevai Leummi (IZL) with 5,000 men and the Stern Gang (1,000) and there were 32,000 registered in the Heil Mishmar or Home Guard.

This phase of the war was spent consolidating Jewish hold on the areas they inhabited and in smuggling in weapons and equipment. The Arabs sought, mainly in vain, to cut off and starve out isolated Jewish settlements.

Israel had proclaimed its politically independent existence on 14 May 1948 and next day the very limited regular armies of Egypt, Syria, Iraq, Jordan and Lebanon attacked the new state. (Saudi Arabia sent some infantry to operate under Egyptian command.)

On 30 May 1948 the Israeli Defence Forces (IDF) were officially established and had 30,000 men under arms with anti-tank and anti-aircraft guns but no tanks, planes or field artillery.

In the south the Egyptians advanced to Gaza, Beersheba, Hebron and Bethlehem where they linked up with Jordan's Arab Legion around Jerusalem. An amphibious Egyptian force was also landed at Majdal on the Mediterranean coast.

New weapons now arrived in Israel including armoured cars, field guns and Messerschmitt fighters; they were rushed into action and halted the Egyptian advance. The Arab Legion pushed westwards from Jordan towards the coast at Tel Aviv and north west to join up with the Lebanese army coming south and the Syrians pushing south west through the Golan Heights.

On 28 May the Jewish quarter of Jerusalem surrendered to the Arab Legion after desperate IDF efforts to capture Latrun and break through from the west to relieve the garrison in the Holy City had failed.

In the north the Syrian assault on Deganyah was beaten off on 20 May and no further serious fighting occurred here but they did take Mishmar Hayarden north of Lake Kinnaret on 10 June.

A truce was called by U.N. Palestinian mediator Count Bernadotte on 11 June and lasted until 9 July. Fighting resumed until 18 July mainly in the south (where the Israelis broke through to their Negev settlements) and in the centre (where they captured Lydda airport and the surrounding area). In the North the Israelis captured Nazareth and made several smaller gains but failed to take Mishmer Hayarden from the Syrians. A second truce ran from 18 July to 15 October 1948 but was frequently violated by both sides; the first Israeli move was to burst through the Egyptian positions along the Majdal-Hebron road, to isolate the 'Faluja Pocket' and to clear the south of the Gaza strip in 'Operation Ten Plagues'. In the north Arab irregulars were expelled into Lebanon.

From 22 December 1948 to 7 January 1949 IDF Operation Horev cleared the major remaining Egyptian positions in the Negev and along the coastal strip. By now IDF planes had secured general command of the air which proved most valuable in this and future operations. The IDF crossed into Egypt at one point but international political pressure caused them to withdraw again. The Egyptians in the Faluja Pocket held out against all attacks and were permitted to withdraw with full honours of war on 24 February 1949.

Israel was now firmly established and her Arab neighbours signed armistices with her; the latest being Syria on 20 July 1949.

The 1956 Campaign (29 October–5 November)

An arms race had developed in the Middle East with Czechoslovakia supplying Egypt with weapons and with U.S.A. supporting Israel. Britain maintained the Jordanian army but on a much lower scale than that of the two other belligerent states. Egypt nationalized the Suez Canal in 1956 and closed it to Israeli shipping; she also formed a joint Arab military command together with Syria and Jordan.

Egyptian forces in Sinai were now given two tasks: 1—to act against Israel in the east; 2—to protect the Suez Canal (in the west) against expected action from Britain and France who had previously controlled the waterway.

The IDF launched a pre-emptive offensive in Sinai (Operation Kadesh) on 29 October with the aim of destroying terrorist (Fedayeen) bases in the Gaza strip, the Egyptian's army's logistic base in the peninsula and of opening the Gulf of Eilat to Israeli shipping. One of the first acts was the dropping of an IDF airborne battalion near Parkers' Memorial in the west centre of the Sinai peninsula to outflank Egyptian positions in the north east. The rest of this brigade raced via Kuntilla, Thamad and Nakhl to join up with their comrades and block the Mitla Pass on 30 October.

An IDF armoured brigade pushed through Rafa (at the base of the Gaza strip), attacked the Egyptian 3rd Division and by 1 November was at El Arish.

In the centre another IDF formation raced through Abu Aweigila and Quseima for the Khatmia Pass which they reached on 1 November. IDF planes seized air superiority and the Anglo-French assault on the Suez Canal and Egyptian airfields on 31 October completed the dislocation of the Egyptian army which collapsed.

The Gaza strip was cleared and the Gulf of Eilat opened; IDF losses were 171 killed, about 1,000 wounded and four captured. Egyptian personnel losses were 6,000 dead and wounded, 6,000 captured and vast quantities of stores and equipment were taken or destroyed.

Israel subsequently evacuated Sinai and the British and French left the canal zone but Egypt's military potential had been ruined for years.

Arab material losses were quickly replaced by the Soviets but the morale of the army took much longer to heal.

The Six Day War 5–10 June 1967

Following the 1956 war a U.N. force was stationed along the Sinai border to act as a buffer between Egypt and Israel, and at the Straits of Tiran to ensure free access to that waterway. The terrorists of the Palestine Liberation Organization (PLO), having been evicted from the Gaza strip, moved their operational bases into Syria and Jordan. Syria had moved into the Soviet camp and her forces were equipped with Soviet weapons. Egypt's President Nasser began to whip up anti-Jewish feeling in the Arab world but made a vital mistake for at this time he had about 60,000 Egyptian troops deployed in the Yemen fighting for the republicans there against the royalists. His available forces in Sinai were thus limited to about 100,000 men and 1,000 tanks. On 17 May he demanded that the U.N. withdraw their forces from Sinai and this was done; on 22 May he closed the Straits of Tiran to Israeli shipping and the IDF was ordered to prepare the now-familiar, crushing pre-emptive strike.

Air superiority was again the key factor and early on 5 June IDF planes mounted a series of low flying raids (to avoid detection by enemy radar) and completely destroyed the air forces of Egypt, Syria and Jordan for the loss of only 19 planes. At 8 a.m. that day IDF Southern Command (three armoured 'divisional' task forces) rushed into the Egyptian positions in Sinai in a near repeat of the 1956 advance. Again, the IDF by-passed enemy positions in order to race for and hold the three vital passes (Giddi, Mitla and Khatmia) to cut off enemy withdrawal and to block reinforcement and resupply. Having disposed of the Arab air forces the Israelis then put their planes into a ground support role and they took heavy toll of the retreating columns of Egyptian troops. Smaller IDF forces pushed south to take Sharm el Sheikh on the southern tip of Sinai on 7 June. The fighting in the Gaza strip was fierce but was over by 7 June by which time the passes had been secured and the Suez Canal reached in the north near El Qantara.

In the Jerusalem sector the IDF attacked Jordanian positions around the city and captured the place on 7 June. They then proceeded to clear all Jordanian troops from the Samarian triangle and the west bank of the Jordan.

The IDF had adopted a quiet role on the Golan Heights until forces were available from the other sectors and on 9 June they had been sufficiently reinforced to attack the Syrian army with the main thrust going in in the northern sector around Tel Azizyat. The fighting was hard but by 2.30 p.m. next day they had broken the Syrian defence and captured Quneitra on the road to Damascus. A U.N.-sponsored cease fire now came into force and the Six Day War ended. Losses for the IDF were 777 killed, 2,586 wounded and some prisoners; the Arabs had over 15,000 killed and wounded, 6,000 prisoners and had lost their air forces and hundreds of tanks, guns and large quantities of equipment. Israel refused to give up the territory she had taken and proceeded to integrate the Golan Heights, West Bank and Sinai into the rest of the state and to place settlements in the captured areas.

The Yom Kippur War 6–25 October 1973

In the period 1967–1973 Israel built the Bar-Lev line along the east bank of the Suez Canal and fortified their conquests in the Golan Heights.

Egypt conducted a war of attrition against the Israelis in Sinai and worked feverishly to rebuild and rearm her forces. This task was hampered by her breach with the Soviet Union in 1972 when 20,000 Russian military advisers were thrown out and all supplies to Egypt of Soviet arms and spare parts ceased. Syria managed to heal the breach however and Soviet aid was resumed.

In the two previous wars Israel had attacked first and had destroyed the Arab air forces to gain air superiority for subsequent operations. The Arabs decided that this time they would dictate the time and place of attack and would counter the undoubtedly superior Israeli air force by forcing it to act in a ground support role in areas saturated with Soviet surface to air missiles (S.A.M. 2, S.A.M. 6 and S.A.M.7).

The Israelis had now become so confident that their tanks alone could decide the outcome of ground conflicts that they had formed 'divisions' and brigades containing only tanks and lacking the conventional infantry and artillery support. They were to pay very heavily for this error.

The balance of forces at the outbreak of the war was:

	Divisions	Men	Tanks	Combat Planes	S.A.M. Batteries
Israel	11	270,000	1,700	500	60
Egypt	12	260,000	2,000	600	650
Syria	7	120,000	1,600	300	200
Iraq	3	30,000	400	60	?

Saudi Arabia and Morocco each contributed an infantry brigade.

The date chosen for the attack on Israel was 6 October—the Jewish feast of atonement. The Bar-Lev Line was only lightly garrisoned and was only designed as a trip-wire defence with two tank brigades in support but it had an extensive buffer zone (the Sinai) behind it whereas the Golan Heights were much closer to the Israeli heartland. When the simultaneous Egyptian and Syrian assaults came at 2 p.m. that day, it was soon clear to the IDF that they could afford to fight a holding action in Sinai while achieving a decision in the vital Golan area.

Syria attacked with three mechanized infantry divisions, two armoured divisions and two armoured brigades on Quneitra and Rafid and were initially opposed by two infantry battalions and two armoured brigades with eleven artillery batteries in support. The IDF planes, trying to stop these thrusts, suffered heavy losses from S.A.M. and from Z.S.U.-23-4 A.A. guns and by 7 p.m. 6 October the 'Barak' Israeli tank brigade had been destroyed, the defences pierced and Syrian armour began to roll towards the Sea of Galilee.

Israeli reserve formations were rushed forward to stem the flood, now only 7 km. from Galilee and, as the Syrians ran out of momentum, the defence strengthened, the Israelis held and on 8 October they were sufficiently reinforced (by three armoured divisions) to mount counter-attacks through Ein Gev and the Gamla Pass. Syrian S.A.M. supplies became exhausted and the IDF gradually gained the upper hand. By 10 October the Syrians had largely been pushed back to their start positions and the Israelis prepared to mount a counter-offensive.

About 8 km. north of Sasa the Syrians had built a strong defensive belt to which they now withdrew but their men were tired and much depleted by the fighting and their ammunition was running low.

On 11 October the Israelis closed up to this line where heavy fighting

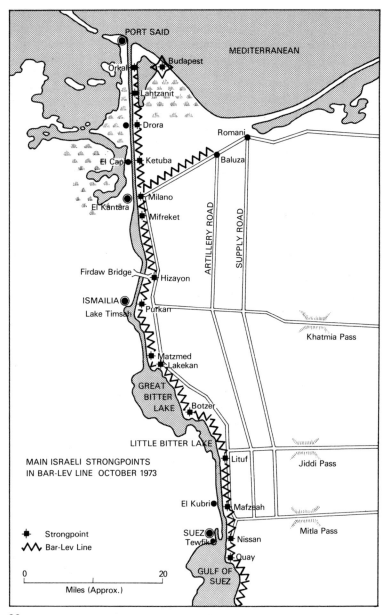

MAIN ISRAELI STRONGPOINTS
IN BAR-LEV LINE OCTOBER 1973

Legend:
■ Strongpoint
〰 Bar-Lev Line

0 — 20
Miles (Approx.)

Map labels:
PORT SAID
MEDITERRANEAN
Orkal
Budapest
Lahtzanit
Drora
Romani
El Cap — Ketuba — Baluza
Milano
El Kantara — Mifreket
ARTILLERY ROAD
SUPPLY ROAD
Firdaw Bridge — Hizayon
ISMAILIA
Lake Timsah — Purkan
Khatmia Pass
Matzmed — Lakekan
GREAT BITTER LAKE
Botzer
LITTLE BITTER LAKE
Lituf
Jiddi Pass
El Kubri — Mafzeah
Mitla Pass
SUEZ — Tewfik — Nissan
Quay
GULF OF SUEZ

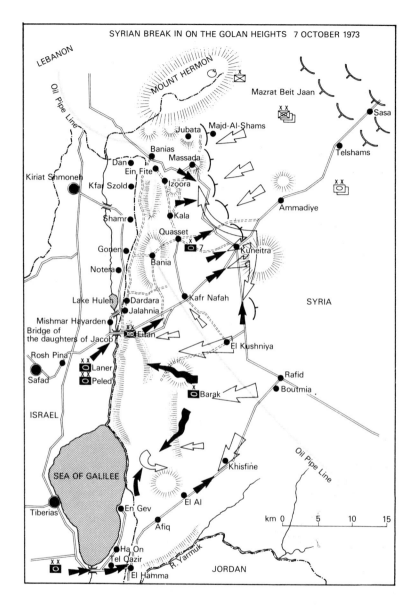

SYRIAN BREAK IN ON THE GOLAN HEIGHTS 7 OCTOBER 1973

LEBANON

Oil Pipe Line

MOUNT HERMON

Mazrat Beit Jaan

Sasa

Jubata   Majd-Al-Shams

Telshams

Banias
Dan   Massada
Ein Fite
Kiriat Shmoneh
Kfar Szold   Izoora   Ammadiye

Shamr   Kala

Quasset
Gonen   Kuneitra
Bania
Notera

SYRIA

Lake Huleh   Dardara   Kafr Nafah
Jalahnia
Mishmar Hayarden
Bridge of   Eitan
the daughters of Jacob   El Kushniya

Rosh Pina   Rafid
Laner   Boutmia
Safad   Peled   Barak

ISRAEL

Khisfine

Oil Pipe Line

SEA OF GALILEE   El Al

En Gev   km 0   5   10   15
Tiberias
Afiq

Ha On
Tel Qazir   R. Yarmuk   JORDAN
El Hamma

33

went on for two days before stabilizing in the defensive belt until 22 October. The Syrians had lost 3,500 dead, 5,600 wounded, 400 captured and 1,000 tanks destroyed, damaged or captured.

The Suez Front
During the night of 5/6 October Egyptian frogmen swam the canal to plant explosive charges in the Bar-Lev sandbank line and to block up the mouths of pipelines designed to flood the canal with blazing oil in case of an assault. At 2 p.m. 16 October the Egyptian Second and Third Armies (two armoured, two mechanized and five infantry divisions plus artillery support from 2,000 guns and fifty S.A.M. batteries) attacked over the canal at three points—south of Qantara, north of Ismailia and south of the Bitter Lakes. About 1,700 tanks were available for this assault and they achieved immediate success. The Bar-Lev Line was washed away with water jets at selected spots to enable the assaulting amphibious tanks to get out of the canal and to push forward into Sinai. Infantry carrying the man-portable SAGGER A.T.G.W. poured across the 70 m. wide canal to form the vital defence screen against Israeli tanks and a dense umbrella of S.A.M. and Z.S.U. 23-4 was erected to act against the IDF air force. The Egyptian air force was held back at this stage so that it could act later in a ground support role in the advance through the three vital passes. The Egyptian plan worked. IDF planes suffered heavy losses against the S.A.M. and Z.S.U. 23-4 and their tanks were decimated by SAGGER fired in salvoes in the open, rolling terrain east of the canal.

While the Israelis mobilized and rushed reinforcements to both Sinai and Golan fronts, it was soon clear that the greatest threat was in the north so the Sinai troops were ordered to just hold on until forces could be released from the Syrian front to enable a counter offensive to be launched in the south.

From 6-14 October the Egyptians extended their bridgeheads in the north (Second Army) and south (Third Army) but did not join them up and this gap was to prove crucial later on. On 14 October the Second Army advanced from its S.A.M. cover to try to seize the vital passes but were repulsed with heavy losses after a fierce battle. A renewed attempt next day fared no better. By now the Golan front had stabilized and the Israelis began transferring forces to the southern front.

On 9 October an Israeli reconnaissance force had crossed the Great Bitter Lake in the gap between the two enemy armies and had found the western shores empty. The IDF seized this opportunity and began to send forces over the canal north of Duwer Soer to strike at the S.A.M. sites from the ground and thus weaken Egyptian air cover over their bridgeheads.

By now the vast majority of the Egyptian armies were on the east bank of the canal and they were unable quickly to transfer forces back to the western side to counter this Israeli raid.

A fierce battle developed at Chinese Farm (on the east bank) as the Egyptians sought to cut off the Israeli thrust on 15 October. They did slow it down but the build up of Israeli forces on the west bank continued and, as more and more S.A.M. sites were destroyed, the IDF air force was able to act more freely over the battlefield and the initiative passed into Israeli hands.

By 22 October the communications of the Egyptians on the east bank of the canal were severely disrupted and Israeli forces had pushed forward and fanned out towards Cairo, Ismailia and Suez.

A ceasefire was agreed upon at 0752 hours that day but it broke down next day because the Israelis wanted to push south to Suez and complete the encirclement of the Egyptian Third Army on the east bank of the canal.

They achieved their aim by 7 a.m. 25 October when a second ceasefire was agreed upon. The superpowers (U.S.A. and U.S.S.R.) had kept the opposing sides supplied with much-needed replacement weaponry and they now managed the ceasefire negotiations.

The fighting was over but this war had shown that the Egyptian and Syrian armies had learned their lessons from the past and had improved their war machines immensely. Israel finished the day in a strong tactical position but had to agree in subsequent negotiations to withdraw from the canal and to give up the three vital passes.

Estimated casualties in this latest Arab-Israeli war were as follows:

	Killed	Wounded	Captured or Missing	Tanks	Fighters	Ships
Israel	2,812	7,500	531	840	120	nil
Egypt	12,000	30,000	9,000	650	182	4
Syria	7,000	21,000	?	600	165	7
Iraq	125	260	18	80	21	nil

Cyprus

After many years of British rule, the Greek-Cypriot majority of the island's population (the minority were of Turkish extraction) began to agitate for independence in 1954. Head of the Greek-Cypriot community was Archbishop Makarios and he approved the setting up of a military wing of the independence movement which became known as EOKA with 'General' George Grivas (who died in January 1974) in command. From 1 April 1955 until 19 February 1959 EOKA mounted a guerrilla war on the British military garrison in the island and numbered at least one serviceman's wife among their kills. Britain exiled Makarios to Mauritius for some time but eventually gave up her control of most of the island following negotiations with Greece, Turkey and the Greek and Turkish Cypriot representatives in Zürich. Ultimate aim of EOKA had been 'Enosis' or political union with Greece but this was firmly vetoed by the Turkish Cypriots and after years of living peacefully together the two communities in the island became increasingly hostile to each other.

Archbishop Makarios (President of the new republic of Cyprus) proposed modifications to the Zürich Agreement and Greeks began to fight their Turkish neighbours on 22 December 1963. British, Greek, Turkish, and later U.N. troops restored an uneasy peace and on 22 March 1965 peace proposals were accepted by Britain and Cyprus but not by the Turkish minority.

The armed truce festered on and on 15 July 1974 there was a Greek-Cypriot coup against Makarios who left the island until 7 December that year, his place being taken by Glafcos Clerides, President of the Cypriot House of Representatives. The Turks, fearing that the coup would lead to Cyprus becoming a Greek province, invaded the island on 20 July and 14 August 1974 with 40,000 troops and secured the northern 40 per cent. of the country. There was a brief period of savage inter-communal fighting with wholesale massacres of men, women and children before all Turkish Cypriots were evacuated into the Turkish part of the island and the Greek Cypriots there were forced out into the south. The situation remains like this to this day. Britain retains two 'sovereign base areas' in the south of the island for national and NATO use (Akrotiri and Larnaca).

Sultanate of Oman

The Jebel Akhdar Campaign (1955-1958)

In December 1955 the Sultan of Oman used his limited armed force to put down a rebellion in the mountainous Jebel Akhdar region in the north of his country. Cause of the trouble had been a Saudi Arabian inspired attempt to cause their puppet—the recently elected Imam Ghalib bin Ali—to break free from the Omani sultans. Egypt and certain U.S. oil interests also supported the uprising. In a swift, small-scale operation the Imam was forced to abdicate but many of his dissident followers fled up to the fertile plateau on top of the Jebel and were able quite easily to block the very few and very narrow access routes to the Sultan's men. The deposed Imam's brother, Talib, fled into Saudi Arabia where he spent two years recruiting more forces and in May 1957 he returned to the Jebel Akhdar and Sharquiya areas to foment new rebellions against the ultra-conservative Sultan. The Sharquiya revolt fizzled out quickly but the Sultan's forces were ambushed as they tried to force the Jebel position and were almost wiped out. Only swift aid from Britain stopped the final defeat of the Sultan and the rebels withdrew up to the top of the Jebel again. For the next two years this stalemate continued while the Sultan's Armed Forces (S.A.F.) were reformed with British aid. They then comprised four regiments of infantry—Muscat, Northern Frontier, Desert and Jebel and were supported by a British artillery battery and a squadron of British armoured cars. S.A.F. now set out to isolate and capture the rebels on the Jebel. Firstly in 1957 the main rebel supply route from Saudi Arabia was cut when Tanuf village was captured and in November of that year the Muscat Regiment discovered an unguarded track up the north side of the plateau. A rapid assault plan was launched and in December Hijar village, half way up the plateau, was captured. The way to the top was still blocked by rebels on the Aqabat al Dhafar—a very strong position—and an assault from the now-unguarded south was decided upon.

On 27 January 1958, part of Northern Frontier Regiment, two squadrons of 22nd S.A.S. and one squadron of the Life Guards rushed rebel positions in Habit village and moved on to occupy rebel head-quarters in Sharaijah. With only light casualties on both sides the rebellion had been terminated.

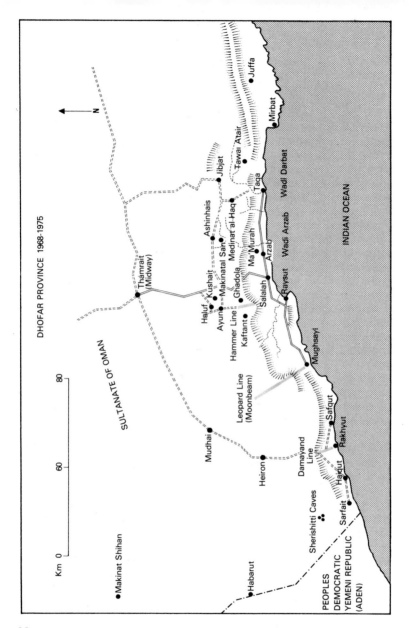

DHOFAR PROVINCE 1968-1975

Makinat Shihan

SULTANATE OF OMAN

Thamrait
(Midway)

Mudhai

Heiron

Sherishitti Caves

Habarut

PEOPLES
DEMOCRATIC
YEMENI REPUBLIC
(ADEN)

Sarfait

Hajut

Damayand
Line

Rakhyut

Safqut

Mughsayl

Leopard Line
(Moonbeam)

Hammer Line

Kaftant

Haluf

Ayun

Kushait

Makinatal San

Ghadola

Medinat al-Haq

Ashinhais

Jibjat

Mahurah

Arzab

Salalah

Raysut

Taqa

Tawal Atair

Wadi Arzab

Wadi Darbat

Mirbat

Juffa

INDIAN OCEAN

N

Km 0   60   80

The Dhofar Campaign (1963–1976)

Trouble broke out in this southern province of Oman in 1963 when Saudi Arabian backed rebels sought to break away from the medieval rule of Sultan Said bin Taimur. Next year the Dhofar Liberation Front (D.L.F.) was formed and enjoyed wide support for their goal of independence within the province.

They mounted armed attacks on government and oil company targets and attempted to assassinate the Sultan. In 1968 the D.L.F. adopted Marxist Socialist doctrine and changed their name to Popular Front for the Liberation of the Occupied Arab Gulf (P.F.L.O.A.G.). Military operations were intensified successfully and aid was received from China who sent arms, equipment and military advisers.

The coastal town of Rakhyat fell to the rebels in 1969 and they soon controlled most of the inland part of the province. P.F.L.O.A.G. extended their raids into northern Oman and the United Arab Emirates but a turning point came on 11 June 1970 when their attack on the S.A.F. garrison at Izki (in central Oman) failed. This event caused the Sultan's son—Qaboos bin Said—to oust his father and take over the state. Educated in Sandhurst, he was well aware of the backward state of his country and sought to introduce progressive changes to avert revolution. He declared an amnesty for the rebels and introduced many reforms in government, education and health services. Many P.F.L.-O.A.G. rebels accepted the amnesty but the Marxist hardcore of the movement were not interested in peace; in September 1970 they ruthlessly purged their organization which caused a further 201 rebels to surrender to the government by March 1971. These reformed rebels were used as the backbone of the government sponsored Firqat (home guard) and the S.A.F. was expanded.

At this time S.A.F. controlled only the larger towns in Dhofar and their immediate environs. With air support Medinat al Haq and Tawi Atair in the eastern Jebel were occupied but garrisons were withdrawn again from June to September when the monsoon rains severely limited flying.

As much rebel aid entered Dhofar from Aden in the west, in November 1971 'Leopard Line'—a series of outposts running from Mughsayl on the coast north east into the Jebel—was set up with the aim of cutting these supply lines. Leopard Line was also evacuated during the monsoon. During 1972 Chinese aid for the rebels waned but the Soviets replaced them. On 19 July 1972 the rebels launched their last large-scale attack—an unsuccessful assault on the coastal town of Mirbat. They were repulsed and chased up into their mountain hideouts with heavy losses.

By October 1972 rebels had been driven out of all areas east of Jebel Samhan and the 'Hornbeam Line' was set up across their lines of supply from Mughsayl due north to Wadi Qaim. In this line the outposts were linked by barbed wire and minefields. The rebels suffered another setback in December 1972 when eighty of them, with quantities of weapons, were captured in Oman and Abu Dhabi. During the 1973 monsoon S.A.F. garrisons were maintained on the Hornbeam Line and at Jibjat and Medinat al Haq. That at Tawi Atair was withdrawn again. Apart from British troops, there were Jordanian engineers and an Iranian infantry brigade helping S.A.F. to fight the rebels who were now receiving help from the U.S.S.R., Libya, Cuba and Aden. By extending the road system, government aid and control was brought into increasing areas previously held by the rebels who in August 1974 changed their name to the Popular Front for the Liberation of Oman (P.F.L.O.).

On 2 December 1974 the Iranian brigade launched an unsuccessful attack on the rebel main base in caves at Sherishitti and Bait Handob and were then diverted to capture Rakhyut which they did on 5 January 1975. They then built the Damavand Line running north of that town. S.A.F. renewed the attack on Sherishitti in December 1974 and captured part of the complex together with much ammunition.

A rebel regimental headquarters together with much equipment was captured west of the Hornbeam Line on 21 February 1975 and in October of that year a new line of posts, wire and mines was built northwards from Sarfait on the coast. Later that month the Sherishitti caves were captured and the rebels lost their main operations base and began to slip away over the border into Aden. Dhalqut was occupied by S.A.F. on 1 December 1975 and the rebellion was practically over.

Since then there have been periodic outbreaks of artillery fire from within the People's Democratic Republic of Yemen (the old British colony of Aden) but Dhofar is pacified and under Omani control.

The Belgian Congo

In the wake of the 'Wind of Change', the Belgian Congo was granted independence, rather suddenly, on 30 June 1960 and was renamed The

Republic of Congo. The Congolese had not been well prepared to take over their own affairs and trouble lay ahead for the infant state. First president was Joseph Kasavubu and the prime minister was Patrice Lumumba. Katanga is a mineral-rich province of the Congo and its president, Moïshe Tschombe, seceded from the union on 11 July 1960, intent on keeping Katanga's riches for purely domestic consumption.

Kasavubu called for U.N. troops to assist in bringing the rebellion to an end but the response to his request was so slow that Patrice Lumumba, apparently on his own initiative, asked Russia to send forces into the country. For this he was deposed, jailed, removed to Katanga where he was murdered in January 1961. Tschombe engaged white mercenaries to lead his native troops and their exploits have brought them a fame and notoriety which lured hundreds to follow their example even as late as 1976 in the civil war in Angola where some of them are still in jail. It took three operations by U.N. troops to end the Katangan secession and Tschombe negotiated his return to the fold in January 1963; he became prime minister one year later. On 1 August 1964 the title of the state changed to the Democratic Republic of the Congo and on 27 October 1971 it was renamed Zaire. In November 1964 a revolt broke out in Kisangani province and many Belgian civilians were taken hostage and held by the rebels in Stanleyville. Belgian paratroops made a dramatic and successful dash into the chaotic city to save these hostages and bring them out. Tschombe was dismissed by Kasavubu in October 1965, but one month later Kasavubu himself was ousted by Lieutenant Colonel (now General) Mobutu. There have been white mercenaries operating in Africa since the Congo but it was here that their reputation was made.

The Biafran Secessionist War

Nigeria contains many 'sub-groupings' of widely differing ethnic backgrounds and while the British had maintained peace during their rule, when independence came these old divisions erupted again. In 1945, 1953 and 1966 there had been massacres of Ibo tribesmen living in the northern region by the Moslem Hausas, who inhabit the north. The mainly Catholic Ibos came from the Eastern Region with its capital at Enugu and after the latest outrages the 'immigrants' began to withdraw from the north and the west into their home area. Lieutenant Colonel 'Jack' Gowon (trained at Sandhurst) became Nigerian head of

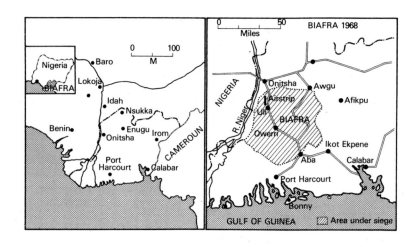

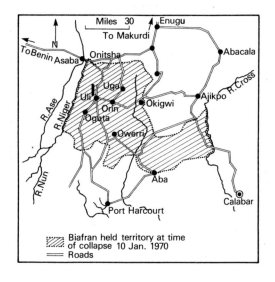

Biafran held territory at time
of collapse 10 Jan. 1970
Roads

state in place of General Ironsi, who was assassinated in 1966. The Ibos declared their secession from Nigeria on 30 May 1967 and an independent republic of 'Biafra' was set up with Lieutenant Colonel Odumegwu Ojukwu (formerly military governor of Nigeria's Eastern Region) as president. The Federal authorities then had 7,000 men, 50 armoured cars, 20 Dornier light planes and 6 Alouette helicopters; the Biafrans were able to muster 5,000 men, 2 B 26 planes and 6 Alouettes. Britain supported the Federal authorities but the Biafrans secured arms supplies from a variety of sources. During June 1967 there were sporadic clashes and on 14 July two Federal battalions took Nsukka. The Biafran 'Air Force' raided Lagos and the Federal army advanced on Enugu and Calabar. Bonny (in the Biafran oilfields) fell on 25 July and that same day the Biafran 120 ton ship *Ibadan* was sunk.

A Biafran counter-attack into the Western Region made great headway however, Yoruba western troops in the Federal forces mutinied and on 9 August 1967 Benin fell to be followed on the 13th by Okene. The Yorubas negotiated with the Ibos to form an alliance against the Hausas but in September and October the Federal army retook the mid-Western Region and entered Biafra, recapturing Enugu, Asaba and Calabar. On 22 March 1968 Onitsha fell; on 19 May Port Harcourt was captured and Biafra was cut off from the sea. Limited resupply was still possible by air into the Uli airstrip but Biafra's fate was now sealed.

This slow strangulation of the infant state continued with the Ibos defending fiercely every foot of territory.

The civilians suffered terrible hardships as the siege went on for the next two years but all to no avail. General Ojukwu fled from Biafra early in January 1970 leaving Major General Phillip Effiong, his chief of staff, to conduct the surrender. Effiong ordered a cease-fire on 12 January 1970 and formally accepted Nigerian Federal authority in Lagos on 15 January.

Angola, Mozambique and Rhodesia

The first shots in Mozambique's struggle for independence from Portugal were fired on 25 September 1964 and soon all Portuguese possessions in Africa were locked in deadly guerrilla wars with support for the terrorists coming from the usual Soviet, Czechoslovakian and Chinese sources as well as from Cuba in the latter stages. In Mozambique it was F.R.E.L.I.M.O. (Frente de Libertacao de Moçambique) which fought the Portuguese; in Angola it was U.N.I.T.A. By 1974 the Portuguese positions in her territories in Africa had become untenable and she withdrew; this precipitated the Portuguese revolution and the introduction of parliamentary democracy to that country. Aid for the guerrillas came not only in the form of weapons and equipment but also in training in the U.S.S.R. and other countries and the provision of bases in countries surrounding Angola and Mozambique.

Since Southern Rhodesia's Unilateral Declaration of Independence (U.D.I.) in 1965 there has been a growing terrorist campaign against that state, aided by the U.S.S.R.

Kenya and Aden

Kenya achieved independence from Britain on 12 December 1963 after suffering an emergency of some years in which a tribal terrorist group—the Mau Mau, based mainly on the Kikuyu tribe—sought unsuccessfully to gain control of the country. Mau Mau developed in the late 1940s and gradually became more active in terrorism until a state of emergency was declared in Kenya in October 1952 and the British army stepped in to help the civil police restore order.

That same month, Jomo 'Burning Spear' Kenyatta (president of the Kenyan African Union since 1947) was convicted of being head of Mau Mau and spent the next nine years in prison. By mid 1956 Mau Mau had been crushed and the fighting ended but the state of emergency continued until 1959. Casualties in this vicious civil war were Kikuyu—11,500 dead (most of these were killed by Mau Mau in its attempts to gain control of the tribe); 95 Europeans, 29 Asians and 1,920 Africans died fighting Mau Mau. Jomo Kenyatta proceeded to become Kenya's prime minister in May 1963 and president in 1964.

After many peaceful years of British colonial rule Aden began to agitate for independence in the 1960s. Just prior to the British evacuation on 30 November 1976, the Adeni terrorist group, National Liberation Front, crushed its other guerrilla rival the Front for the Liberation of South Yemen (F.L.O.S.Y.) and the British-inspired South Arabian Federation of seventeen Sultanates around Aden collapsed. The old colony became the People's Democratic Republic of Yemen (P.D.R.Y.).

1. Private, Motor Rifles

3. Woman Junior Sergeant

2. Senior Sergeant

4. Private, Motor Rifles

6. Junior Sergeant,
   Airborne Troops

5. Senior Sergeant

7. Artillery Major

9. Private, Motor Rifles

8. Junior Tank Lieutenant

10. Warrant Officer, Medical Corps, U.S.S.R.

12. Lieutenant, Motor Rifles, Bulgaria

11. Lance Corporal, Motor Rifles, Bulgaria

13. Engineer Major, Bulgaria

15. Lance Corporal, Motor Rifles, Czechoslovakia

14. Sergeant Major, Paratroops, Bulgaria

CZECHOSLOVAKIA

16. Corporal, Airborne Forces

18. Staff-Sergeant, Airborne Forces

17. Major, Motor Rifles

19. Sergeant, Czechoslovakia

21. Infantry Private, East Germany

20. Private, Guards Regiment,
East Germany

22. Tank Major, East Germany

24. Major General, Hungary

23. Corporal, Military Police, Hungary

25. Corporal, Signals, Hungary

26. Infantryman, Hungary

27. Private, Mountain Troops Poland

POLAND/RUMANIA

28. Tank Crewman, Poland

29. Sergeant, Paratroops,
Poland

30. Woman Musician,
Rumania

31. Corporal, Mountain Troops

33. Private, Motor Rifles

32. General

34. Lieutenant, Tank Troops
     Rumania

36. Senior Warrant Officer,
     Mountain Infantry,
     Yugoslavia

35. Corporal, Yugoslavia

37. W.R.A.C. Sergeant,
    Military Police

39. Gurkha Private

38. Private, Light Infantry

GREAT BRITAIN

40. Infantry Subaltern

41. Paratrooper

42. Infantryman

43. Infantryman

44. Infantryman

45. Infantry Corporal

46. Sergeant Major, Denmark

48. Dutch Officer

47. Infantryman, Denmark

49. Infantryman

50. Nurse (S.A.S.)

51. Paratrooper

52. Algerian National Liberation
    Army (ALN)

54. Algerian National Liberation
    Army (ALN)

53. French Légionnaire

55. Lance Corporal,
    Mountain Troops

56. Corporal, Airborne Troops

57. Staff Sergeant,
    Armoured Fighting Vehicles

ITALY

58. Private, Lagunari

60. Corporal, APC Infantry

59. Lance Corporal, Bersaglieri

61. Lieutenant of Engineers

63. Trooper, Armoured Troops

62. Corporal, African Forces

64. Regimental Sergeant Major
Mountain Infantry,
Austria

65. Sergeant, Light Infantry,
Canada

66. Infantry Captain,
U.S.A.

67. Commanding General

68. Infantry Sergeant

69. Supreme Commander

70. Sergeant Farrier,
Switzerland

71. Adjutant, Infantry,
Belgium

72. Paratrooper, Spain

73. Infantry NCO, Sweden

75. Infantryman, Finland

74. Infantry Sergeant Major,
Norway

BRITISH COMMONWEALTH IN KOREA

76. Sergeant, Indian Army

77. Infantry NCO, Australia

78. Company Sergeant Major, Canada

79. Warrant Officer, North Korea

80. Infantryman, China

81. Infantryman, China

82. Infantry Lieutenant,
    Republic of Korea

84. Infantryman, Turkey,
    UN Forces

83. Machine-Gunner, Republic of Korea

85. Gurkha Corporal,
    UN Force

86. Mercenary Officer,
    Katanga

87. Mercenary Soldier,
    Katanga

NIGERIAN CIVIL WAR 1967–68

88. Biafran Major General

89. Nigerian Infantryman

90. Nigerian Infantry Sergeant

91. Lieutenant Colonel,
    Zambian Signals

92. Regimental Sergeant Major,
    Zambian Rifles

93. Lance Corporal,
    Commando Brigade,
    Biafra

REPUBLIC OF SOUTH AFRICA

94. Major, Special Service
    Battalion

96. Infantry Patrol Commander,
    South West Africa (Namibia)

95. Corporal, Women's Service

97. Signaller

99. Private Rhodesian African Rifles

98. Lance Corporal, Selous' Scouts

RHODESIA

100.   Major, Grey's Scouts, 1978

101. National Guardsman,
Panama

102. Cavalry Sergeant, Brazil

103. Brazilian Infantryman

INSURGENTS

104. Soldier, Malayan Races
     Liberation Army

106. Mau-Mau General, Kenya

105. EOKA Soldier, Cyprus

107. Paratroop Corporal

108. Tank Corps Major

109. Officer, Territorial
Defence Corps

EGYPT

110. Paratrooper

111. Major General

112. Infantryman

113. Christian Militiaman

114. Christian Militiaman

115. Muslim Irregular

116. Lieutenant Colonel, Engineers
Saudi Arabia

118. Sergeant, Tank Troops, Iran

117. Artillery Sergeant, Lebanon

119. Infantry Corporal, Syria

121. Major, Signals, Abu Dhabi

120. Guardsman, Muscat

122. Iranian Infantryman

123. Second Lieutenant,
Trucial Oman Scouts

124. Corporal,
Sultan of Muscat's
Armed Forces

125. Gurkha Corporal, Nepal

127. Major General, Pakistan

126. Major, Artillery, Nepal

128. Infantry Sergeant, Pakistan

130. Signaller, India

129. Lieutenant, Airborne Artillery,
India

131. Légionnaire

132. Colonial Paratrooper

133. Tirailleur Algérien

134. Viet Cong Guerrilla,
North Vietnam

135. ARVN Ranger,
South Vietnam

136. Infantry Private,
North Vietnam

137. Infantry Sergeant,
     North Vietnam

138. Lieutenant Colonel,
     Infantry, Mongolia

139. Staff Sergeant,
     Military Police,
     Taiwan

140. Specialist

141. Paratrooper

142. Sergeant,
U.S. Special Forces

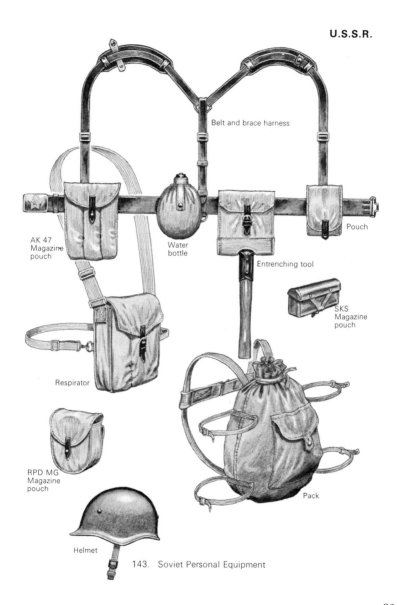

Belt and brace harness

Pouch

AK 47
Magazine
pouch

Water
bottle

Entrenching tool

SKS
Magazine
pouch

Respirator

RPD MG
Magazine
pouch

Pack

Helmet

143. Soviet Personal Equipment

U.S.S.R.

144. Armoured troops

145. Armoured troops

146. Airborne troops

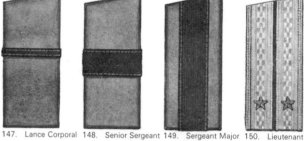

147. Lance Corporal 148. Senior Sergeant 149. Sergeant Major 150. Lieutenant 151. Major

152. Armoured troops

153. Gunners

154. Motor Riflemen

155. Junior other ranks

156. Length of Service.
Other ranks

144/156. Soviet Insignia

94

157. APS (*Stetschkin*) 9 mm. pistol

158. SKS (Self Loading
Carbine Simonow)

159. AK 47
(*Kalaschnikow*)

160.
RPD (*Roschnoi
Pulemet
Detjarew*)

157/160. Soviet Infantry Weapons

161. Officers' field
service cap

162. Other ranks' side cap

163. Tropical hat

164. Fur cap

165. Military police
helmet

166. Paratroopers' beret

167. Paratroopers' jump
helmet

168. Tank crewmen's
helmet

161/168. Soviet Headdress

169. Polish
field cap

170. Polish
mountain troops

171. Hungarian
field cap

172. Czechoslovakian
field cap

169/172. Polish/Hungarian/Czechoslovakian Headdress

173. Yugoslav mountain trooper

174. Major,
Summer Combat Dress

175. Soldier,
Rubber NBC Suit

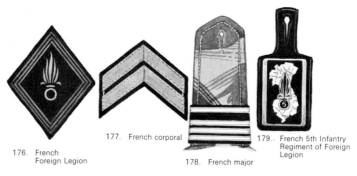

177. French corporal

176. French
Foreign Legion

178. French major

179. French 5th Infantry
Regiment of Foreign
Legion

182. Polish cap badge

181. Bulgarian shoulder
board (sergeant major)

183.
DDR
shoulder strap
(corporal)

184.
DDR
shoulder strap
(junior sergeant)

180. Bulgarian shoulder
board (junior
lieutenant)

185. Hungarian
cap badge

186. Yugoslavian
shoulder strap
(sergeant)

187. Yugoslavian
shoulder strap
(junior sergeant)

188. Rumanian
mountain corps.

100

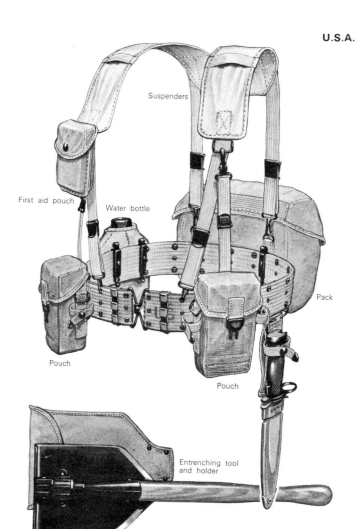

Suspenders

First aid pouch

Water bottle

Pack

Pouch

Pouch

Entrenching tool
and holder

189. United States Personal Equipment

U.S.A.

190. Private First Class

191. Sergeant Major

192. Specialist 5th Class

193. Captain's combat badge of rank

195. Combat dress

PRESLEY

194. Fatigue dress name tag

196. Fatigue dress

197. Airborne and Special Forces

198. 1st Air Cavalry Division

190/198.   United States Army Insignia

199. M 60 Machine-Gun

201. M 14
Self loading
rifle

200. M 16
Self loading
rifle

199/201. United States Infantry Weapons

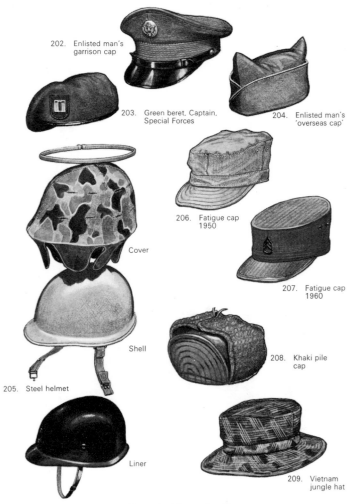

202. Enlisted man's garrison cap

203. Green beret, Captain, Special Forces

204. Enlisted man's 'overseas cap'

Cover

206. Fatigue cap 1950

207. Fatigue cap 1960

Shell

208. Khaki pile cap

205. Steel helmet

Liner

209. Vietnam jungle hat

202/209. United States Headdress

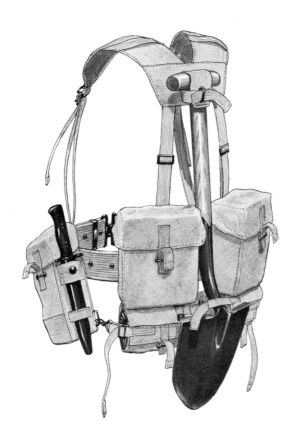

210. Web Equipment 1958 Pattern

GREAT BRITAIN

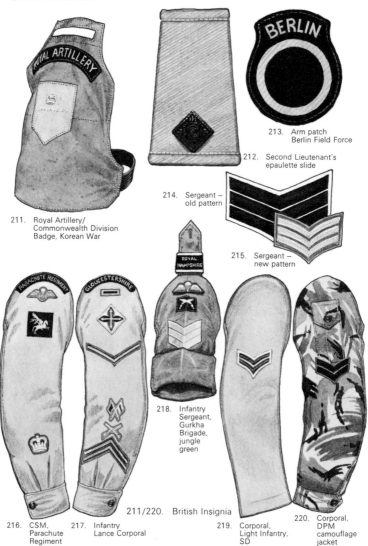

213. Arm patch
Berlin Field Force

212. Second Lieutenant's
epaulette slide

214. Sergeant –
old pattern

211. Royal Artillery/
Commonwealth Division
Badge, Korean War

215. Sergeant –
new pattern

218. Infantry
Sergeant,
Gurkha
Brigade,
jungle
green

211/220. British Insignia

216. CSM,
Parachute
Regiment

217. Infantry
Lance Corporal

219. Corporal,
Light Infantry,
SD

220. Corporal,
DPM
camouflage
jacket

106

221. FN
Machine-Gun

224. Sterling
Sub Machine-Gun

222. FN
Self loading
rifle

223. Individual
Weapon (IW)
(Bullpup)

221/224.   British Infantry Small Arms

225. Jungle hat

226. Gurkha hat

227. Infantry beret (Gloucestershire Regt)

228. SAS beret

229. Steel helmet with visor

230. DPM combat hat (1970)

231. Combat cap (1950)

232. Wessex Brigade (Gloucestershire Regt)

234. Cavalry beret (9th/12th Prince of Wales' Own Royal Lancers)

235. Para jump helmet

225/235. British Headdress

236. Bomb Disposal Officer

Glass-reinforced
plastic helmet with visor

Non-slip shoulder pad

Armoured vest

Shield

Riot baton

Leg shields

237. British Body Armour

WEST GERMANY

239. Hauptfeldwebel's shoulder strap slide

240. Unterleutnant

241. 1st Luftlande – Division, arm patch

238. Oberfeldwebel, combat suit

ITALY

242. Parachute Brigade, arm patch

243. Warrant Officer, shoulder strap

244. Major, shoulder strap

245. Sergeant Major Folgore (Airborne) Division

ISRAEL

246. Corporal

247. Staff Sergeant (combat only)

248. Lieutenant

238/248. Insignia, Various Nations

111

250. French MAT 9 mm.
Machine-Pistol
M-1949

249. French 7.5 mm.
M-1949/56 MAS

251. Israeli 9 mm.
UZI Sub
Machine-Gun

252. Israeli 5.56 mm.
GALIL Assault
Rifle

249/252. French and Israeli Weapons

254. Czechoslovakian 7.65 mm.
M-61 Skorpion
Machine-pistol

253. West German
7.62 mm.

255. Australian 9 mm.
F-3A1 Sub Machine-Gun

253/255. Various Small Arms

113

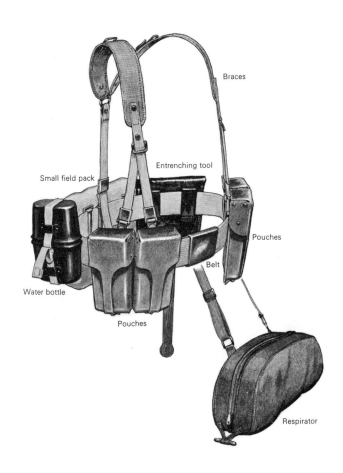

Braces

Entrenching tool

Small field pack

Pouches

Belt

Water bottle

Pouches

Respirator

256. West German Personal Equipment

257. Muleteer, Mountain Artillery

258. French Foreign Legion
junior ranks

259. French paratrooper's
combat hat

260. West German Mountain
Troops,
field cap

261. Malayan Races
Liberation Army

258/261. Miscellaneous headdress

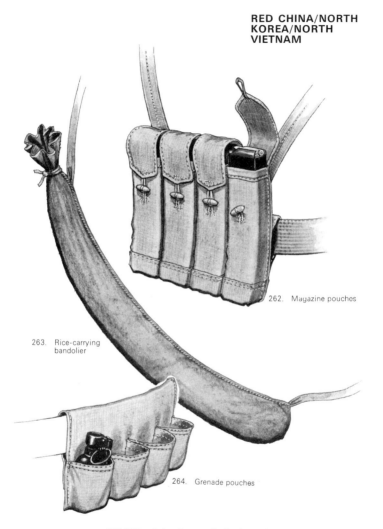

262. Magazine pouches

263. Rice-carrying
bandolier

264. Grenade pouches

262/264. Asian Communist Equipment

265. British DMS boot

266. U.S. field boot

267. French patrol boot

268. West German
Mountain Troops
boot

269. South African
DMS boot

265/269. Boots

270. British jungle boot

271. Viet Cong jungle boot

272. U.S. Vietnam service

270/272. Boots

1. U.S.S.R.: Private, Motor Rifles, Summer Field Dress, 1945-70.
This is the uniform made famous in the great battles of World War II. The Gymnastjerka blouse was worn as fatigue and combat dress up until the new uniforms were introduced for the Soviet Army in the 1971-72 period. The small ammunition pouches are for the SKS rifle (see plate 158). Until quite recently the Russians wore foot cloths and not socks in their boots.

2. U.S.S.R.: Senior Sergeant Lightweight Tropical Uniform, 1965-79.
The Soviet army has a large area of operations in Central Asia in which the extremely hot summers certainly call for special clothing. Apparently shorts were considered to smack too much of colonialism to be adopted for the People's Army! The shoulder board ranks have been retained unaltered in the new uniforms. Jack boots and breeches were also worn with this form of dress until about 1960 as was a lightweight Gymnastjerka.

3. U.S.S.R.: Woman Junior Sergeant, Summer Service Dress, 1945-70.
During World War II women frequently fought and died alongside the men in the Red Army, but nowadays they are employed on clerical, administrative, culinary and signalling tasks as in most other armies. For parades the beret was dark blue and a single-breasted, khaki, four-button fronted jacket with brown gloves were worn. Summer field uniform was the khaki beret and shirt, no tie, Sam Browne belt, khaki shirt and jackboots.

4. U.S.S.R.: Private, Motor Rifles, Winter Field Dress, 1945-70.
Until 1971 Motor Rifles (Infantry) wore magenta facings on collar patches, shoulder boards and on piping and band of the peaked cap. After this date their facings changed to red. The fur cap seems to be worn with the earflaps firmly up regardless of the weather. His weapon is the ubiquitous AK47 (whose characteristics are given in plate 159) and his equipment pouches are different from those on the first figure because of the different magazines used.

5. U.S.S.R.: Senior Sergeant, Summer Field Dress, 1945-70.
The familiar Gymnastjerka is here decorated with the long service badge on the right breast (red banner over gold star and wreath, white,

triangular pendant with the number of years' service in black; silver wings) and two medal ribbons on the left breast; the white ribbon with two red stripes is the Order of the Red Banner, instituted in 1918 and awarded for outstanding courage or long service both on an individual and collective basis; the orange ribbon with three black stripes is the medal for Victory over Germany in the 1935-45 war. On the shoulder boards is the small regimental badge in matt bronze.

6. U.S.S.R.: Junior Sergeant, Airborne Troops, Summer Service Dress, 1970-79.

This jaunty, somewhat nautical costume was the 1970 replacement for the Gymnastjerka. Airborne troops, facings are shown on the beret, collar patches, shoulder boards and on the new arm patch. The facings of other corps of the Soviet Army are: tank troops, signals, engineers, artillery, transport, NBC and pipeline troops—black, medical—red, veterinary and administration—dark green.

7. U.S.S.R.: Major, Artillery, Summer Service Dress, 1972-79.

In the period 1970-72 considerable confusion reigned as to which facing colours were to be worn, artillerymen and others often appearing with red hat bands instead of their own colour. When the new uniforms had been fully introduced they received black hat bands with red piping. A new rank was also introduced at this time; this was the Praportschick or warrant officer. His shoulder boards were in the facing colour with two gold stars. With the introduction of the arm badges, interesting combinations could be seen on the uniforms of specialists attached to battalions. Transport corps drivers serving with infantry units for instance would wear black collar patches with transport badges but the motor rifles' red arm patch.

8. U.S.S.R.: Junior Lieutenant, Tank Crew, Summer Combat Dress post, 1972.

Members of tank crews wear black overalls, khaki shoulder boards and a small, yellow tank (of the same design as that on the arm patch) embroidered on the right breast. The crews of other armoured fighting vehicles wear the same helmet and overalls but no tank badge and wear their coloured regimental shoulder boards with gold CA if applicable.

9. U.S.S.R.: Private, Motor Rifles, Summer Suit, 1975.

With his 'skeleton order' NBC satchel and entrenching tool, this man carries an RPD light machine-gun of which details are given on plate 160.

10. U.S.S.R.: Warrant Officer, Medical Corps, Summer Parade Dress, 1972-80.

The Russian army wore dark green uniforms long before the Napoleonic era and in 1970-71 the colour was reintroduced for parade dress, khaki being retained for everyday wear. We see here the new warrant officer's rank stars on the colour-of-arm backing. Note that the medical corps' facings changed from dark green to red. The badges on the lower sleeve show years of service as follows: 1 thin chevron—1 year; 2—2 years; 3—3 years; 1 thick chevron—4 years; a star over a thick chevron—5 to 9 years; two stars over a chevron—over 10 years. The medical corps badge is a snake coiled over a goblet all in gold.

11. Bulgaria: Lance Corporal, Motor Rifles, Winter Combat Dress, 1968-79.

From 1945 to 1950 regiments in the Bulgarian Peoples' Army expressed their identity purely by facing colours (with gold or silver lace for officers) shown on collar patches and shoulder boards: infantry—red (and gold), paratroops blue piped red (and gold); field artillery black piped red (and gold); AA artillery black piped blue (and gold); self propelled artillery black piped red (with zig zag pattern on gold lace); tanks red piped yellow (and silver); cavalry red piped white (and silver); medical and veterinary—blue (and silver); engineers—black piped red (and silver); general staff officers—black edged red and silver; technical services—violet (and silver).

In 1968 badges were introduced for the various arms and they are remarkably similar to those of the Soviet forces except that the silver motor rifles badge has crossed rifles under the star. The collar badges of long service motor rifles' NCOs are red with black edging; those of conscripts brown with red edging. The weapon is the AK47 (see plate 159); the equipment Soviet pattern but the helmet is similar to the Wehrmacht coal scuttle.

12. Bulgaria: Lieutenant, Motor Rifles, Summer Combat Dress, 1968-79.

While soldiers wear a plain red star with brass edging on their caps, officers and senior NCOs wear an oval silver cockade with white-over-green over red centre bearing a red star.

All ranks wear the white-green-red shield on the side of the forage cap.

13. Bulgaria: Major, Engineers, Summer Walking Out Dress, 1968-79.

The engineers' facing colour (black) is shown on collar badges and shoulder boards as is the silver badge of crossed axes. For parade dress a brown leather Sam Browne belt would be added and the trousers and shoes would be replaced by breeches and jack boots.

14. Bulgaria: Sergeant Major, Paratroops, Summer Camouflage Uniform.

While most Bulgarian combat troops wear the field grey, paratroops have the camouflage suit shown here. He carries the short AK47 MPi with the collapsible butt.

15. Czechoslovakia: Lance Corporal, Motor Rifles Summer Combat Dress.

Throughout this book various patterns of camouflage clothing, all for use in roughly the same terrain, will be seen. It is interesting to speculate as to who has the right (or best) answer! After using the Soviet helmet for some time, the Czechs have produced their own version, rather similar to that worn by the German army from 1939-45. The badge of rank is well concealed—it is the small grey 'button' on the patch on the right breast. The weapon is the AK47 (see plate 159), the equipment Soviet pattern.

16. Czechoslovakia: Corporal, Airborne Forces, Summer Combat Dress, 1965-79.

Corporals wear two grey 'buttons', junior sergeants three, sergeants one silver star, staff sergeants two, company sergeant majors three (in a triangle), the three grades of warrant officer wear one, two and three stars in a horizontal line between silver bars top and bottom. Officers wear gold stars (1 to 4 up through captain; 1 to 3 between horizontal gold bars for major through colonel); gold stars with sequins between horizontal gold braid for major general, lieutenant general and colonel general. The light, plastic helmet was introduced for airborne forces in 1965.

17. Czechoslovakia: Major, Motor Rifles, Winter Dress.

The long parka is added over summer dress for winter use and a grey, Soviet-pattern pile cap would be worn in extreme cold. In service and parade dress rank badges are worn on the shoulders by all ranks and brass collar badges denote regiment. These are after the Soviet pattern except that AA artillery has its own badge—an airplane flying across an upturned gun barrel. Generals wear gold lime leaves embroidered on red backing on their collars.

18. Czechoslovakia: Staff-Sergeant, Airborne Forces, 1950-65.

This plate shows the old camouflage pattern replaced in 1965 by the subdued grey-green style.

19. Czechoslovakia: Sergeant, Summer Duty Wear.

The waist-length blouse is summer wear common to most Warsaw Pact States and is a comfortable, practical item.

20. East Germany: Private, Guards Regiment, Parade Dress, 1972.

This elite unit the 'NVA Wachregiment' as the cuff band proclaims—mounts guard daily in East Berlin at the Memorial to the Victims of Fascism on the famous Unter den Linden. Not only is the goose step unchanged from 1939 but every detail of the uniform, down to the pattern of the silver lace loops on cuffs and collar, are exactly as they were in the Wehrmacht. He carries the Soviet SKS rifle (see plate 158), retained for use with ceremonial troops because it lends itself to a good 'present arms'.

21. East Germany: Infantry Private, Summer Combat Dress, 1978.

The personal equipment is a replica of the black leather Wehrmacht items but in grey webbing with pouches modified to take AK47 magazines. These weapons are produced in East Germany, frequently with brown plastic butts and pistol grips. The helmet was designed for the Wehrmacht in 1944 but not introduced into service until about 1952.

22. East Germany: Major, Tank Troops, Walking Out Dress, 1972.

Once again, World War II buffs will recognize all items shown. The facings were pink for 'Panzers'; buff for infantry; black for engineers;

lemon yellow for signals; dark red for artillery; black for technical troops; blue for rear services. Badges of rank are also almost exactly as they were from 1939-45.

23. Hungary: Corporal of Military Police.

Hungarian and Finnish are languages which share almost nothing with any of the other languages which surround them. The F on the helmet equates to the Cyrillic P worn by the Soviet 'Regulators' or traffic police. The protective clothing obscures such uniform detail as facings and badges but the two stars on the helmet denote a corporal. Facings are worn on collar patches, piping and band to peaked cap, and on officers' shoulder boards; they are black for tanks, red for artillery and green for infantry, engineers, signals, medical, technical, transport and administration. Regimental badges in brass are worn on these collar patches; examples are; infantry—crossed rifles; tanks—a tank; field artillery—crossed gun barrels on three balls; AA artillery—as before but on a pair of wings; transport—a lorry within a cog wheel. He carries an AK47 with folded butt.

24. Hungary: Major General, Summer Walking Out Dress, 1970.

Hungary's extreme climate warrants special summer clothing like this smart lightweight white coat. The British army wore similar tunics in the tropics. The elaborate cap badge is the green-white-red national cockade surmounted by the red star. In about 1974 new parade and walking out uniforms were introduced for the army and all ranks were worn on the shoulder strap as follows: Lance corporal one bronze star; corporal two; sergeant three; staff sergeant a narrow gold bar under a star; company sergeant two stars and a bar; battalion sergeant three stars and a bar; junior warrant officer a star over a narrow and a wide gold bar; senior warrant officer as before but two stars. Junior lieutenant a star on a gold stripe; lieutenant a star; senior lieutenant two stars; captain three. Field officers have the lower part of the shoulder strap covered in gold lace with one, two and three stars (major through colonel), generals have all gold shoulder straps and one to three silver stars (major general, lieutenant general and colonel general).

25. Hungary: Corporal, Signals, 1945-71.

This NCO (recognized by the two white stars on his collar patches is in summer parade uniform with its peculiar brown leather gaiters. The signals collar badge is a circle enclosing a 'T' with six lightning flashes radiating from it. Winter dress includes the Soviet-pattern grey pile cap (with red-white-green oval cockade and red star) and jack boots.

Junior ranks wear rank and regimental badges on their collar patches, officers wear their regimental badge under a gold button on their collar patches and wear the stars of their rank on their shoulders. In 1974 an arm badge was introduced for all ranks; to be worn on the upper left arm in service dress and in shirt sleeves; it was a khaki shield, outlined in white and bearing the white letters MN.

26.   Hungary: Infantrymen, Summer Camouflage, pre-1970.
The helmet and RPD machine-gun (see plate 160) are Soviet and so is the personal equipment. This camouflage suit was replaced in 1970 by the subdued grey-green combination. The value to the Warsaw Pact of the Hungarian army has not been tested since the bloody Soviet repression of the Hungarian uprising in 1956.

27.   Poland: Private, Mountain Troops, Winter Field Dress, 1945-79.
These specialist soldiers are deployed in the mountains in the South of Poland. Polish ponies are used for transport purposes; it is doubtful if they can carry as much as a good mule. The present Polish cap badge bears a strong resemblance to that worn by the army of the Duchy of Warsaw from 1807-1813.

28.   Poland: Polish Tank Crewman, Winter Combat Dress, pre-1969.
In 1969 the Soviet-pattern cloth tankers' helmet was replaced by a Polish designed black plastic item with brown leather ear and neck piece. The black leather suit is relatively water resistant, has good fire-retardant properties and is readily available; thus combining many of the virtues demanded by tankers of the western world.

29.   Poland: Sergeant, Paratroops, 1975.
The red beret, international symbol of the airborne forces, is decorated here with the Polish eagle and the badge of rank. Rank is also worn on the shoulders of the summer combat uniform. The helmet is similar to that introduced for tank crew personnel in 1969 but has no fittings for earphones. His weapon is an AK47 MPi with collapsible butt.

30. Rumania: Woman Musician, 1972.

As in many armies, women are employed in the non-combat sections of the Rumanian People's Army. Bands wear red facings and on their shoulder boards is a brass lyre.

31. Rumania: Corporal, Mountain Troops, 1973.

The collar patches show the facing colour—green. Facings for other corps are crimson for cavalry; black for tanks, artillery, technical troops, transport, engineers and signals; red for infantry and rear services; crimson for medical troops. On the shoulder straps are the rank badges (gold bars on the facing colour) and the corps badge—here a stylised sprig of fir. The weapon is the AK47 MPi with a collapsible butt.

32. Rumania: General, Summer Service Dress, 1972.

General officers have their own collar badges (gold oak leaves), hat badges and shoulder boards, and red piping to cuffs, red side stripes to trousers.

33. Rumania: Private, Motor Rifles, Summer Camouflage, 1975.

Here is yet another pattern of camouflage for the European summer flora! In 1974 the Rumanians replaced the Soviet helmet with their own pattern (shown here) which is very similar to that worn by the Rumanian army in 1939. The weapon is an AK47 (see plate 159).

34. Rumania: Lieutenant, Tank Troops, Summer Parade Dress 1974-79.

Here again is the new Rumanian helmet; for parade purposes an enamelled metal badge (the national cockade) is affixed to the front. The gold shoulder boards bear a silver tank, and are edged in the facing colour with a central stripe in the same colour. The pocket badge is awarded for attending a course at the war college.

35. Yugoslavia: Corporal, Summer Combat Dress, 1978.

The helmet has a distinct Wehrmacht flavour, the equipment is Soviet pattern but his 7.62 mm. machine-pistol is the Yugoslav-produced M-56, modelled on the German 9 mm. MP 40. (See half tone plate 172 for details.) The rank badges are all worn on the shoulder strap; one red chevron for lance corporal; one gold sergeant; two staff sergeant; three company sergeant; four junior warrant officer; one narrow over one wide—senior warrant officer.

There are four grades of lieutenant, the two junior being shown by small brass stars; the senior two by one and two large stars respectively; junior captain three stars; senior captain four. Field officers have gold edging to shoulder straps as well as the stars as follows: major—one; lieutenant colonel—two; colonel three. General officers have the gold edging and the stars above a gold laurel wreath enclosing crossed swords; major general—one star; lieutenant general—two; colonel general—three; army general—four; general—five.

36. Yugoslavia: Senior Warrant Officer, Mountain Infantry, Summer Parade Dress, 1972.

The cross strap of the Sam Browne is worn here in a novel but very practical way, supporting the pistol on the right hip. This pistol is a locally produced 7.62 mm. 'M-67' weapon with an eight round magazine; effective range 30 M.; muzzle velocity 420 m./sec. using the Tokarew cartridge. The brass collar badges are crossed rifles on a wreath. Other corps' badges are: artillery—crossed gun barrels; armour—a head-on view of a tank; ordnance—a cog wheel on which are a gun barrel crossed on a key behind a tank with a vertical adjustable spanner behind them; medical—a snake on a staff; veterinary—as before but with a letter v in the centre; NBC—crossed retorts; bands—a lyre; signals—crossed lightning flashes; engineers—an anchor behind a bridge with a wreath formed half of laurels (*left*) and half a cogwheel (*right*).

37. Great Britain: WRAC Sergeant attached to the Military Police in Northern Ireland, 1973.

Members of the Women's Royal Army Corps serve with a number of corps including Royal Signals, Intelligence Corps and Royal Army Ordnance Corps. In Northern Ireland they form a vital part of the search teams and as such are constantly exposed to attack. They are not armed and are deliberately distinguished by the bright red cap with Military Police badge (a Military Police collar badge is worn on the left breast). To protect them they wear the standard body armour vest which protects reasonably well against 9 mm. projectiles but is of very limited value against high powered rifles or the M 60 machine-gun.

38. Great Britain: Private, Light Infantry, Riot Order, Northern Ireland, 1972.

Since this figure was 'in action' a new, lighter combat helmet has been introduced for the British army in the province. It is of glass reinforced plastic with improved ballistic protection over the steel helmet pictured here. It also sits much more securely and has built-in bump protection which the old helmet lacked. His 38 mm. riot gun can be used to fire tear gas grenades or baton rounds (rubber bullets). The batons can be either a single projectile or three smaller, thick discs designed to be used at very close range (about 10 m.) against crowds of rioters. The trousers are standard 1970 pattern DPM, the gaiters '37 pattern webbing. His hat badge is the silver, stringed bugle always associated with light infantry.

39.   Great Britain: Private, 6th Queen Elizabeth's Own Gurkha Rifles, Winter Combat Dress, Denmark, 1963.

Following the granting of independence to India in 1947, four regiments of Gurkhas were retained with the British Army; the 2nd King Edward VII's Own (The Sirmoor Rifles), the 6th, the 7th Duke of Edinburgh's Own and the 10th, Princess Mary's Own. At any one time three of them form the Gurkha Brigade which is normally stationed in Hong Kong and the fourth serves in the United Kingdom. They have not been employed in Northern Ireland. The cap badge includes the legendary Gurkha Kukri. He wears the 1960 Parka and the 'Cold Weather Warfare' boots with special thick soles and thermal insoles. His dark green gloves are regimental dress items, other units wearing khaki.

40.   Great Britain: Second Lieutenant, Devon and Dorsets, 1971.

To confuse snipers it is standard practice for officers as patrol leaders to carry the same weapons as the men, hence the SLR (see plate 222). He wears regimental cap badge (silver castle) and shoulder strap slip ons with one, four-pointed star over the regimental title all in black; 1958 pattern webbing and 1970 pattern DPM (Disruptive pattern material) trousers with puttees and DMS boots.

41.   Great Britain: Private, 3rd Battalion, The Parachute Regiment 1971.

With the famous red beret we see the Denison Smock (now being replaced by a DPM smock), lightweight olive green trousers, 1944 pattern webbing and puttees. On his shoulder brace a field dressing has been fixed on with 'jungle tape'. His weapon is the 84 mm. Carl Gustav, produced in Sweden, firing a hollow charge projectile with an effective range against tanks of 400 m. The green arm patch denotes 3rd Battalion; the 1st wears red; the 2nd blue.

42. Great Britain: Private, 1st Battalion Royal Hampshires, Malaya, 1954.

The yellow hat badges are battalion and company recognition devices (here 'A' Company); he wears the Gurkha Brigade arm patch, modified '44 pattern web equipment with a belt made of parachute-drop harness, jungle boots and carries the Australian pattern sleeping bag. His weapon is the Australian 9 mm. Owen Gun with 24.7 cm. barrel, 33 round magazine, 700 rpm, effective range 75 m.

43. Great Britain: Private, 1st Battalion Gloucestershire Regiment, 1957.

This soldier is shown in battledress (which was worn from 1939 to 1962) and is in 'Internal Security (IS) Order' with helmet, shield and pick axe helve for crowd control. The helmet is painted in regimental gloss black and on the back is the regiment's back badge (awarded for the Battle of Alexandria). At the top of the sleeve is the U.S. Presidential Citation, awarded to this regiment and to 'C' Troop, 170th Independent Mortar Battery, Royal Artillery, for their heroic stand against overwhelming Chinese odds near Solma-ri on the Imjin river in Korea on 23, 24, and 25 April 1951. The diamond patch below is the Wessex Brigade badge, the cross of Athelstone.

44. Great Britain: Private, Black Watch, Hong Kong, 1972.

Instead of the beret worn by English regiments, this Scottish regiment wears the highland bonnet with khaki tourie and red hackle over the regimental badge.

He wears tropical olive drab shirt and trousers with the Hong Kong dragon sleeve patch and 1944 pattern web equipment which was found to be most useful for jungle use because it absorbs very little water and thus does not weigh much more wet than dry. His weapon is the Sterling SMG (see plate 224 for details).

45. Great Britain: Corporal, Queen's Own Regiment, Hong Kong.

The blue diamond on the jungle hat is a company recognition badge and he wears the temperate service khaki flannel shirt, favoured by some regiments for tropical wear. With the '44 pattern web equipment he carries a U.S. M 16 A1 carbine, well suited for jungle use.

46.   Denmark: Sergeant Major, Service Dress, 1975.
Prior to 1969 the Danish army wore British-style khaki but the smart, rifle green and grey was introduced in that year. On the side of the cap is the army badge (three rampant lions on a crowned shield scattered with hearts—all in a laurel wreath) and on the collar the regimental badge (here the three rampant lions within a laurel wreath and under the cypher 'C4' of the Sjaellandske Livregiment). On the buttons is the infantry corps badge—crossed rifles over a shovel all under a crown. The crimson backing of his collar badges indicates regimental HQ: 1st Battalion wears red backing, 2nd white, 3rd yellow and 4th blue.

47.   Denmark: Infantryman in Combat Order, 1974.
The combat dress and webbing are Danish, the helmet and the M 1 7.62 mm. Garand rifle are U.S. pattern. The weapon weighs 4.37 kg. unloaded, is 1.105 m. long with a 61 cm. barrel, 300 m. effective range, gas operated, 24 rpm, 850 m./sec. muzzle velocity and an eight-round magazine. It is unusual that the trousers are worn loose at the bottoms.

48.   Netherlands: Lieutenant, Stoettroepen, Service Dress, 1974.
Rank is worn on the shoulder straps (up to about 1968 it was worn on the collar patches) and consists for officers of gold stars; for junior officers (1 to 3) stars (over a gold bar for field officers). Regimental identity is expressed by the hat and collar patches and the brass badges on them; Stoettroepen having a sword between antlers. On the left arm is the Netherlands lion holding a sword and a bunch of arrows over the scroll JE MAINTENDRAI. He wears parachutist's wings. In the Dutch army tank troops wear black berets, other troops wear khaki.

49.   France: Private, Line Infantry Algeria 1956-61.
In this bitter war Algeria gained her independence from France in the post war era of European colonial decline. The bush jacket can be worn inside or outside the trousers. The walking stick was a popular item with the men on long patrols in the rough country. The weapon is the MAS 36 (Manufacture d'Armes de Saint-Étienne) 7.5 mm. rifle.

50.   France: Nurse, attached to 'Sections Administratives Spécialisées (SAS), Algeria, 1958.

The SAS were an intelligence unit employed in 'hearts and minds' operations in close contact with the Algerians. She wears airborne pattern camouflage trousers and the French canvas and rubber patrol boots with a green scarf on the shoulder—the temporary field recognition badge of the column of French infantry and Algerian harkis that she is operating with. The 12-bore shotgun is for personal protection.

51.   France: Private, '3 Régiment de Parachutistes Coloniaux', Algeria, 1957.

This was one of the units of General Massu's airborne division which cleared the Algiers casbah of terrorists in the spring of 1957 with a thoroughness equalled only by the ruthlessness with which they completed the task. He wears French airborne camouflage suit and well polished jump boots, U.S. webbing and carries the French 9 mm. MAT (Manufacture d'Armes de Tulle) '49, blow back machine-pistol. It weighs 3.63 kg. empty (4.23 kg. with 32-round magazine), length 40.6 cm. with butt folded (66.1 cm. with it extended); barrel length 22.8 cm., effective range 100 m., rate of fire 600 rpm, muzzle velocity about 380 m./sec. The fighting knife does not double as a bayonet. The close haircut is typical of this élite, hard fighting unit.

52.   Algeria: ALN (National Liberation Army), 1960.

American clothing, equipment and weapons found their way into many hands after the war, including the ALN as shown here by the 1943 pattern jacket, the webbing and the Thompson .45 inch, blowback operated sub machine-gun. Magazines holding 20 or 30 rounds are available; the weapon fires 700 rpm, effective range 90 m., muzzle velocity 280 m./sec. making the weapon a very low grade threat. Algeria had been ruled by France for 150 years before achieving independence by force of arms in 1962 after seven years of bitter fighting. President de Gaulle conducted a referendum in France and Algeria which resulted in a majority for breaking the connection between the states and acted on this mandate. This made him extremely unpopular with certain sections of the French army who set up the OAS, a terrorist group dedicated to frustrating Algerian independence and to killing de Gaulle.

53.   France: Légionnaire, Compagnies Sahariennes Portées de la Légion Etrangère, 1959.

The Algerian Saharan sun has scorched the face of this latter day Beau

Geste. On his sleeve is the black and dark green badge of the infantry of the Foreign Legion and he wears the unmistakable képi here in a sand cover and with goggles as protection against sand storms. The wide scarf helps keep the sand from mouth and nose. He carries a U.S.-made 7.62 mm. M-1 Winchester, semi-automatic carbine; length 90.4 cm., barrel length 45.7 cm.; weight 2.37 kg. empty (2.7 kg. with full 15 round magazine); rate of fire 30 rpm.; effective range 150 m.; muzzle velocity 610 m./sec. There were four of these companies operating vigorously over the southern Sahara and the ALN were not successful in whipping up support in this region.

54. Algeria: National Liberation Army, 1960.

Once again a picture of international flavour with the British BD blouse, French infantry camouflage trousers and Wehrmacht MG 34. This blow back weapon was produced in Germany, Austria and Czechoslovakia during World War II; it was originally made by Mauser, had a calibre of 7.92 mm., length 1.219 m., barrel length 62.7 cm.; effective range 800 m., rate of fire 800-900 rpm., muzzle velocity not known. The weapon can be fed by belts of 50 or 250 rounds or it can use drum magazines holding 50 or 75 rounds. It weighs 12.1 kg. unloaded.

55. West Germany: Gefreiter (Lance Corporal), Mountain Troops, 1972.

The Federal German Armed Forces (Bundeswehr) were formed in 1956 and initially wore uniforms which seemed to have been designed by a rabid pacifist to make the wearers look ridiculous.

Dress in the German army has undergone many changes since then and the combat dress particularly is well designed and functional. All ranks wear the national flag on both sleeves, the mountain troops (one division of three brigades deployed along the country's southern border) wearing the same Edelweiss cap badge as was worn during World War II. The Alpenstock climbing rope and mountain boots with thick stockings, canvas gaiters and breeches enable the men to move well in the mountains.

56. West Germany: Corporal (Unteroffizier), Airborne Troops, 1976.

This NCO is wearing the red beret with silver plunging eagle cap badge with its oak wreath surround and the reddish-brown summer combat suit. The green loop across the bottom of the shoulder strap (on which his badge of rank appears) indicates infantry. Other colours are pink—armour; black—engineers; red—artillery; lemon yellow—signals; blue—logistics; crimson—NBC; deep yellow—reconnaissance. He carries full marching order with sleeping bag on his pack, respirator in the green plastic satchel, 'NATO' helmet and MP 5 A 3, 9 mm., blow back machine-pistol with collapsed butt. The weapon is also used by the German Police and Border Guards. It weighs 2.45 kg., is 68 cm. long with butt extended; barrel length is 22.5 cm., effective range 100 m., rate of fire 650 rpm., muzzle velocity 400 m./sec. Magazines can hold 10, 15 or 30 shots. The weapon is made by Heckler and Koch.

57. West Germany: Oberfeldwebel (Staff Sergeant), Armoured Fighting Vehicle Crewman, 1975.
Tank crewmen in the German army wear black berets with a bronze badge of a tank emerging from an oak wreath (this badge is often, unofficially, backed with pink silk—the tankers' facing colour). The crewmen of other armoured fighting vehicles (SP artillery, Armoured Recovery Vehicles, light reconnaissance vehicles, APCs) wear the red-brown beret with national cockade over crossed sabres shown here. All wear the one-piece 'Panzerkombination' or tank overall, with the jack boots known as 'Knobelbecher' (dice cups).

58. Italy: Private, Lagunari, 1977.
The Lagunari are a type of marine force designed to operate in the shallow coastal waters around Venice and other river estuaries (hence the lifejacket). The beret badge shows a mural crown over an anchor over crossed rifles and the man wears a regimental cravat. The camouflaged kit is well known in Britain where much of it is imported for leisure wear! His canvas and rubber boots are specially designed for his amphibious role. He carries the Beretta 7.62 mm. BM-59 SLR. Length 1.095 mm. (1.235 m. with bayonet); weight 4.41 kg. (5.63 kg. with 20-round magazine); effective range 300 m., gas operated, 800 rpm.; muzzle velocity 840 m./sec.

59. Italy: Lance Corporal, Bersaglieri, 1975.
Italian army uniforms have changed only very little since before World War II; as a reminder of their African colonial service, the Bersaglieri (famous as light infantry and for their 'run-past' on parades) wear a fez off parade or the bush hat with flowing, black cocks' feather plumes on formal occasions. Even on the Italian pattern steel

helmet they wear this parade plume as the Alpini (mountain troops) wear a black pompom and eagle's feather on their steel helmets. On the collar of the camouflage jacket is the white star of Savoy. Rank badge (a black chevron) and divisional sign appear on a detachable brassard on the left arm. He carries the Italian produced BM-59 7.62 mm rifle.

60.   Italy: Corporal, APC Infantry, 1978.
The lightweight plastic helmet gives bump protection and communications facilities; uniform details as for previous figures. When not wearing specialist headgear like tank helmets, berets are worn in regimental colours as follows; Bersaglieri, armour and SP artillery—black; airborne—maroon; field artillery—khaki; Alpini wear traditionally their famous mountain hat with eagle's feather.

61.   Portugal: Lieutenant, 1st Engineer Regiment, Service Dress, 1960.
This severe, smart grey uniform is worn for parades. The cap badge has the national crest under a red cross and resting on flags over the regimental number (1) and the corps badge—a silver castle. The collar patches are in the corps colours and bear the castle, the buttons are matt gold. Badges of rank appear on the cuff. Other regimental badges (in brass) are: cavalry—crossed lances; infantry—crossed rifles; artillery—crossed gun barrels.

62.   Portugal: Corporal, African Force, 1964.
Angola, Mozambique and Guinea were considered by the Portuguese as part of Metropolitan Portugal but this constitution could not resist the anti-colonialist mood of Africa and by 1976 they had been granted independence after a prolonged guerrilla war heavily supported by the communist bloc. This native NCO's uniform reeks of the colonial past with its fez, shorts and puttees; rank appears on the shoulder straps. Sergeants have three gold chevrons point down, staff sergeants three point up; company sergeant majors four point up and regimental sergeant majors wear the silver national crest within a gold laurel wreath. Officers wear gold bars—1-3 for lieutenant to captain; the same system over a wider gold bar for major, colonel; brigadiers wear two, five-pointed silver stars, major generals three and lieutenant generals four. Generals have red collar patches with gold oak leaf embroidery.

63.   Portugal: Trooper, Armoured Troops, Angola, 1973.

135

The black beret bears the crossed lances and regimental number in brass but the tropical combat kit is suitably anonymous. French patrol boots were found to be useful in this environment and apart from issued weapons many soldiers carried their own fighting knives according to taste and pocket.

64. Austria: Oberstabswachtmeister, Mountain Infantry, 1976.
The familiar Edelweiss cap badge of World War II Wehrmacht pattern is complemented by a Rucksack of similar design vintage. Rank is worn on the shoulder strap and is also indicated by the design of the hat cockade. A corporal wears two stars, junior sergeant three; sergeant a star over a silver bar; staff sergeant two stars and bar; company sergeant one star over a wide and a narrow bar; regimental sergeant major two stars and two bars; junior warrant officer three stars and two bars; senior warrant officer one silver star over a wide gold bar. The Alpenstock, climbing rope, breeches, stockings and boots are international mountaineering equipment; the Austrian 7.62 mm. SLR has integral bipod legs for greater stability when firing.

65. Canada: Sergeant, Princess Patricia's Canadian Light Infantry, 1975.
The Canadian Brigade in Germany is now deployed in the South of Germany with the American army, having previously been stationed with the British army in the Soest area until about 1970. National identity is shown by the flag on both sleeves, ranks are as in the British army for soldiers but a new system of navy-style gold bars was introduced for officers at the time of the unification of Canada's defence forces in 1968. On the shoulder strap is worn the regimental title (here PPCLI) in light buff woven letters.

66. U.S.A.: Captain, Infantry, Korea, 1953.
This helmet cover is an old sandbag and the boots are suede leather. Two types of hand grenade are attached to the flak jacket and the whole figure oozes fatigue.

67. U.S.A.: General Ridgway, Korea, 1952.
After a distinguished career in World War II, General Ridgway took over command of the U.S. Eighth Army in the crisis of a withdrawal on 23 December 1950 when the U.N. forces were being pushed south from the Chinese border by half a million Chinese 'volunteers' fighting for

the North Koreans. On 11 April 1951, when General Douglas MacArthur was sacked by President Truman for disagreeing with the 'No attacks across the Yalu River' doctrine, General Ridgway assumed command of all U.N. forces in Korea. On the peak of his fur combat cap he wears the four stars of his rank over the parachutist's wings.

68.   U.S.A.: Infantry Sergeant First Class, Japan, 1953.
This man is probably in Japan on 'Rest and Recuperation' from service in The Korean War as evidenced by the 'Butcher's Apron' as the blue and white striped U.N. medal ribbon for that conflict is known in the British army. Here it is worn at the outer, lower end of the rows of ribbons. On his right chest he wears the U.S. Presidential Unit Citation— at the time America's highest collective award for bravery in the field. His collar badges bear the infantry crossed rifles and the blue badge half hidden under the lapel is the infantry combat badge. The bottle of PX Bourbon concealed behind his back would ensure a warm welcome anywhere in Tokyo.

69.   U.S.A.: General Alexander Haig, Supreme Commander Allied Powers in Europe, 1975.
In October 1975 the Federal German Army held a Corps exercise called 'Grosse Rochade' up against the Czechoslovakian border and General Haig, while visiting a German Fallschirmjäger battalion was presented with one of their maroon berets with its plunging eagle badge which he wore for the rest of his visit. As an old infantryman he wears the infantry combat badge on the left breast.

70.   Switzerland: Sergeant Farrier, Dragoons, 1973.
This mounted unit (Switzerland's last) was disbanded in 1973. Under the peculiar Swiss 'citizen army' system, the troopers provided their own horses and received an allowance for their fodder and upkeep. The horses were frequently transported by rail through the mountains to the desired area of operations. Despite having a relatively small army, the Swiss have a bewildering variety of badges to indicate regiment (the collar patches), regimental number (the shoulder strap slide), company within the regiment (the coloured band under the regimental number), specialist trades (the arm shield—here Farrier), rank (under the arm shield) and awards for achievements (over the left breast pocket—here marksman).

71. Belgium: Adjutant, Infantry, Service Dress, 1978.

The light khaki service dress is very similar in style to that of the British army and an Adjutant, as senior warrant officer, wears many officers' appointments such as the gold hat badge of the infantry of the line (repeated on the shoulder straps). The badge of the 3rd Parachute Battalion (on the right pocket) signifies that this man served with that unit in Korea as part of the U.N. forces. On the right sleeve is the elementary parachutist's badge.

72. Spain: Private, Spanish Parachute Brigade, Jump Gear.

This shows a fairly standard paratrooper's uniform, the unusual feature being the brigade badge (the Spanish eagle and the parachute) worn on the front of the parachute pack. The Spanish army uses its own 7.62 mm. SLR, the CETME (Centro de Estudios Técnicos de Materials Especiales) as seen in West Germany and many other states. Machine-pistols are the 9 mm. STAR blowback weapons with 10 or 30 round magazines, rate of fire 450 rpm, muzzle velocity 380 m./sec.

73. Sweden: Infantry NCO, 1960 Pattern Service Dress.

On the front of the cap is the national cockade and on the side the regimental badge (here a rampant Griffon for the Södermanland regiment. On the collar the crossed rifles of the infantry. Other corps badges worn on the collar are artillery—crossed gun barrels, cavalry—crossed sabres, engineers—a grenade. Generals wear three gold oak leaves on each collar patch. Badges of rank (worn on the left collar patch in combat (kit) are shown for junior NCOs by gold bars—lance corporal—1; corporal—2; corporal quartermaster—3; quartermaster —4; sergeant—one gold disc, staff sergeant—two; sergeant major—3; Officers wear five-pointed gold stars—second lieutenant—1; lieutenant —2; captain—3; major—1 star under a crown; lieutenant colonel—2 stars under a crown; colonel—3; senior colonel—4. Generals have golden shoulder straps with crossed batons under stars—major general —1; lieutenant general—2; general—3. All ranks through colonel wear the regimental number at the base of the shoulder strap.

74. Norway: Sergeant Major, Infantry, winter combat dress, 1970.

National identity is expressed by the hat cockade and the national flags on the upper arms. Although NCOs now wear their rank badges on the shoulder straps in combat kit, the badges themselves have not changed and are as for the British army for lance corporal, corporal, sergeant and officers up through captain. Staff sergeants have three stripes under a bar; field officers have silver edging to shoulder straps and from one to three silver stars for major through colonel. Major general through general have silver shoulder slides with from one to three larger stars. On service dress and battle dress officers wear their ranks on the collar. The weapon is the German 9 mm., blow back 'MP 40' of World War II vintage. It weighs 4.03 kg. (4.7 kg. with 32 round magazine), is 63 cm. long with butt folded (83.5 with it extended); barrel length is 25.1 cm., effective range 100 m.; rate of fire 500 rpm, muzzle velocity 390 m./sec.

75. Finland: Infantryman, Camouflaged Combat Suit, 1970.

The Finnish army still uses the old Wehrmacht World War II helmet and produces many of her own small arms, infantry weapons and ammunition. This man carries the M-44, 7.62 mm. Mosin-Nagant carbine with five round magazine—muzzle velocity 770 m./sec., barrel length 52 cm., effective range 300 m. In combat dress badges of rank are worn on an eight-sided tab on the right wrist, junior ranks wearing yellow chevrons (point up), officers wearing thick and thin gold bars. In service and working dress rank badges are worn on collar patches which are in the regimental colours as follows: infantry—green with white edging; field artillery—red with blue; coastal artillery—red with blue; AA artillery—red with white; logistics—blue with white; pioneers—crimson with white; veterinary—lemon yellow with blue; medical—grey with red; air force—blue with black; dragoons—deep yellow with blue; signals—dark crimson with yellow; anti-tank artillery—black with red edging.

76. Indian Army: Sergeant, 60th (Parachute) Field Ambulance, 1952.

The turban (here in crimson, regimental colour) uncut beard and steel bracelet on the right wrist (not visible in this plate) denote a Sikh soldier, much respected as a martial race. Badges of rank in the Indian and Pakistani armies have remained as they were under British rule except that the crown of British army ranks has been replaced by the three lions and the star and crescent respectively.

77. Australia: Corporal, 3rd Bn, Royal Regiment, 1953.

The famous bush hat of this 'Digger' is unmistakable in any environment. On the brassard is the U.S. Presidential citation over the Commonwealth Division patch over his rank badges. The Australian army rank badges are as for the British army as are most of the corps badges. He wears both the British and U.N. Korean medal ribbons.

78. Canada: Company Sergeant Major, Royal (Can.) Army Service Corps, 1951.
Canadian battledress was slightly darker in colour than the British equivalent and was made of finer cloth. Corps badges and rank badges were as for the British army at this time except that Warrant Officers 1st class wore the Canadian crest on their forearms instead of the royal arms of the United Kingdom.

79. North Korea: Warrant Officer, Summer Dress, 1952.
The similarity with the Soviet Army of the period is striking as would be expected when it is remembered that from 1945 to 1952 the U.S.S.R. trained and equipped the North Korean army. For that reason the rank badge system was almost identical and the Soviet Gymnastjerka blouse can be recognized here. Small arms were of Soviet pattern as were artillery pieces and tanks.

80. China: Infantryman, Winter Combat Dress, Korea, 1950.
Although very few distinguishing marks were worn on this quilted cotton clothing, the Red Chinese army of this period had a system of rank and regimental badges somewhat similar to that of the Soviet army. Officers and Warrant officers wore shoulder boards on parade dress but in working and combat dress they wore their badges on the collar patches. He carries a hand grenade and a Chinese copy (known as the 'Type 50') of the Russian 7.62 mm. blowback sub-machine-gun PPsh M-41. The U.N. forces in Korea christened it the 'Burp Gun'. It weighed 3.64 kg. (5.4 kg. with 71 round drum magazine; its length was 83.8 cm., barrel length 26.5 cm.; effective range 100 m.; rate of fire 900 rpm; muzzle velocity 500 m./sec. Most Chinese weapons of this era were straight copies of Soviet equipments.

81. China: Infantryman, Summer Field Marching Order, Korea, 1951.
Partly to conceal their identity, many of the Chinese troops in Korea did not wear their regimental collar patches or their red star cap badges. Chinese equipment is characterized by simplicity and functionality.

The wooden pack frame allows the load to be rested at a moment's notice and forms a convenient section of a tent frame. The collar patches were red for soldiers of all corps except airforce and airborne forces (who wore light blue) and navy and public security (also part of the army) who wore black. The patches bore' yellow stripes and silver stars (to the front) to indicate rank and the corps badge at the rear (infantry had no corps badge). These badges were cavalry-crossed sabres; armoured troops—side profile of a tank; artillery—crossed gun barrels; pioneers—crossed pick axe and shovel; signals—a disc bearing a lightning flash, aerial mast and telephone; airborne—a winged parachute; transport—side profile of a lorry; medical—a round disc bearing an upright cross; administration—a round disc bearing a five-pointed star; railway construction—a stylised railway crossing; maintenance—crossed spanner and pliers. Rank badges were as follows; privates and lance corporals had plain red patches with one and two five-pointed silver stars respectively. Corporal, sergeant and senior sergeant had a yellow stripe along the centre of the patch and from one to three silver stars respectively. Officer cadets had red patches edged yellow; warrant officers—yellow patches with no stars. Junior officers had red patches with a single gold line along the centre; they wore from one to four silver stars from second lieutenant through senior captain. Field officers were as above but with two gold stripes and from one to four, larger, silver stars from major through lieutenant, junior and senior colonels. Generals' collar patches were edged gold and their silver stars were even larger—from one to four for major general through lieutenant, colonel and senior general. Marshals had one larger silver star under the Chinese crest; senior marshals had a pine frond wreath around the star.

During the cultural revolution (1967-69) all ranks in the Chinese army were abolished as were the badges and all personnel now wear plain red collar patches.

82. Republic of Korea: 1st Lieutenant of Infantry, 1st Division, 1952.

The American influence in the uniform of this young army is unmistakable. The infantry collar badge is a crossed rifle and sabre; on helmet and shoulder straps are the two silver diamonds of his rank. A second lieutenant has one such diamond, a captain three. Major through colonel are shown by from one to three silver flowers each with nine-pointed petals; brigadier general to general wear five-pointed silver stars, from one to four in number. Warrant officers have a golden diamond on the shoulder strap, NCOs wear their ranks on the upper arm or, on certain forms of dress, on yellow edged, light green rectangles on the left breast. Ranks are shown by yellow chevrons (point down) and for senior NCOs these are worn over horizontal yellow bars. Lance corporal—one chevron, corporal—two; sergeant—three, staff sergeant —three over one bar, sergeant first class—three over two bars; master sergeant—three over three bars, first sergeant—as before all under a star.

83. Republic of Korea: Machine-Gunner, Winter Combat Clothing, 1953.

Those who took part in this war know how bitter the winters could be, thus the cocooned appearance. In warmer, more peaceful times, in service dress, the Korean army wears the national crest within a five-petalled silver flower all within a laurel wreath on the peaked cap, the badge of rank on the side hat. Collar badges show the corps badge and these are on a circular disc for other ranks as in the U.S. Army. Examples are: artillery—crossed gun barrels; tanks—the front profile of a tank on crossed sabres; medical corps—a winged staff with entwined snakes; transport—a ship's wheel enclosing a wing; NBC—crossed retorts on a shield; women's army corps—a female head; bands—a lyre. These are all in brass; silver badges are—military police—crossed pistols under a star; quartermaster—a key with wings in a laurel wreath. Other badges are engineers—a castle gate in silver enclosing a gold star; signals—crossed signal flags over a silver torch; ordnance—a gold grenade on three interlocking silver rings.

84. Turkey: Private, Infantry Battalion, Korea, 1952.

The Turks wrought a great fighting reputation for themselves in the war although their identity was only shown by helmet badges and arm patches, their clothing being supplied entirely by the Americans. Badges of rank for soldiers were worn on the upper arms in chevrons (point down); second class private—one red chevron; first class private —two; lance corporal—one yellow chevron with, in its centre a yellow circle enclosing a yellow star and crescent; staff sergeant—four and sergeant major—five. Officers wore gold, five-pointed stars on the shoulder strap, one to three up through captain. Field officers had at the base of the shoulder strap a gold oak wreath closing at the top with the star and crescent and then one to three stars major through colonel. Generals were as for field officers but the wreath was underlaid with silver crossed sabres on a red ground.

85. U.N. Force: Corporal, 5th Gurkha Rifles, 1966.

Nowadays it is the custom that all U.N. troops wear sky blue berets, but in 1964 troops wore their own headdress. At the time of partitition of British India into India and Pakistan in 1947, the 2nd, 6th, 7th and 10th Gurkha Rifles transferred to the British army and the 1st, 3rd, 4th, 5th, 8th, 9th and 11th Regiments continued to serve with the Indian army. This NCO wears British 1937 pattern web equipment and is every inch as smart a soldier as we have come to expect in the British Army. He carried the well known .303 inch (7.7 mm.) Lee-Enfield No. 1 Mark 3 British rifle; weight 3.9 kg. (4.45 with bayonet), length 1.132 m. (1.567 m. with bayonet); barrel length 64 cm.; effective range 400 m.; ten round magazine, 20 rpm; muzzle velocity 745 m./sec.

86. Katanga: Major Mike Hoare, 1964.

During Katanga's brief independence it was white mercenaries like this Britisher who trained and led the province's armed forces by methods as dramatic as they were often unconventional. 'Mad Mike' Hoare led No. 5 Commando and the dark green beret is doubtless related to that of the Royal Marine Commandos. The hat and shoulder badges have a strong Belgian flavour.

87. Katanga: Mercenary Soldier, No. 5 Commando, 1964.

The fluid situation in the Congo attracted many soldiers of fortune for a great variety of reasons. As can be seen, the equipment (and weapons) came from equally diverse sources.

88. Biafra: Major General.

In its brief existence the Biafran army was continually fighting and had little time or effort to expend on the niceties of dress such as uniformity. Men wore what they could get and frequently went without much of what would be regarded as basic essentials. The General wears U.S. style camouflage with British gorget patches and cane and the Biafran army emblem on the upper sleeve. The rank badges were generally as in the British army but we see here two, six-pointed black stars under the Biafran crest in yellow (a spread eagle on an elephant's tusk over three interlocking 'horse shoes').

89. Nigeria: Infantryman.

British, American and Soviet equipment was used by both sides if available; this casualty has a label pinned to him describing wound and treatment given so that should he fall unconscious, the next medic will know what to do.

90. Nigeria: Infantry Sergeant.
The helmet is American and bears a private decoration. These were fairly common during this war and included phrases like 'Jungle Bunny' and 'Killer'. He wears British 1958 pattern web equipment and carries a British Sterling SMG (see black and white plate 224 for details). Rank badges in the Nigerian army were almost identical to those in the British army.

91. Zambia: Lieutenant Colonel, Signals, 1972.
After achieving independence in 1966, Northern Rhodesia became Zambia and at once began the task of 'Zambianising' its government and armed services. By 1972 only half a dozen European officers were left and in the next year they were all replaced by natives. This officer wears signals badges on collar and hat as in the British army except that the crown is replaced here by the Zambian fish eagle (as it is on the rank badges on the shoulder straps). The dark blue lanyard on the right shoulder is also as worn in the Royal Signals; the black hat plume and pugree stripe are regimental distinctions.

92. Zambia: Regimental Sergeant Major, Rifles, 1972.
As a battalion of the 'King's African Rifles' this regiment had worn shorts under British rule but these were replaced by long trousers after independence. The brass, British coat of arms on the right wrist seems to have been retained as the RSM's badge for a little longer however, as was the highly polished pace stick.

93. Biafra: Lance Corporal, 4th Commando Brigade, 1967.
White mercenaries were also active in this war; the brigade commander here being a German named Steiner who had previously served in the Foreign Legion. Under the Biafran sun badge is the skull and bones of the 4th Commando Brigade, one of the army's best fighting units.

94. South Africa: Major, 1 SDB (Special Service Battalion), 1972.
This unit is part of the armoured corps, hence the black beret. South African forces have been involved in several 'hot pursuits' of guerrillas

across their northwest border through South West Africa (Namibia) and into Angola. Rank badges are roughly similar to the British army system but without the crowns.

95. South Africa: Corporal, Women's Service.
The rank chevrons have a distinct Wehrmacht flavour. This corps is employed in administrative, signalling and civil defence tasks.

96. South West Africa (Namibia): Infantry Patrol Commander, 1978.
Here comfort has amended the issue uniform quite heavily and for security reasons he wears no rank badges. Namibia had elections in 1978 and now has a government which—like that of Zimbabwe-Rhodesia—is recognized by practically no one.

South Africa and Rhodesia both actively recruit blacks into the security forces as indeed they must if they are to survive. He carries the N.A.T.O. SLR (see plate 222 for details).

97. Rhodesia: Signaller, 1976.
As can be seen from the rain cape and the mud, this figure is operating in the rainy season. Apart from the usual supporting arms and services, the Rhodesian army contains the following infantry regiments— Rhodesian African Rifles (a black regiment); Rhodesian Light Infantry, Rhodesian Regiment and 'C' Squadron Rhodesian Special Air Service Regiment. Armour is represented by the Rhodesian Armoured Cars Regiment (The Selous' Scouts) and mounted infantry (dragoons?) by the 250-strong Grey's Scouts. Badges of rank are exactly as in the British army except that the crown is replaced by the lion holding an elephant's tusk and the RSM's coat of arms badge is that of Rhodesia.

98. Rhodesia: NCO, Selous' Scouts, 1978.
The camouflage pattern of this unit is very similar to that of the Denison smock worn by British airborne forces in World War II. On his hat front is a black chevron—lance corporal. The badge of this regiment (which has an SAS-type role) is the head of a sable over the motto ASESABI LUTHO the Sindebele for WE FEAR NOUGHT. He carries a N.A.T.O. SLR and wears locally produced webbing and South African boots.

99. Rhodesia: Private, African Rifles, 1976.

The neck flap on the caps is to keep water from running down the men's backs in bush fighting. This regiment distinguished itself in the Burma campaign in World War II by routing the Japanese at Tanlwe Chaung and has recently been increased to two battalions.

100. Rhodesia: Major, Grey's Scouts, 1978.

Students of saddlery will recognize quite the simplest snaffle bridle with no nose band—a far cry from the traditional military double-bitted bridle. The saddle seems to be modelled on the American army McClellan saddle of 1874 which itself was derived from the wooden saddles used by the Turks in the Middle Ages. The rider is U.S. citizen L. H. 'Mike' Williams with the following military career: 1942 enlisted in U.S. Army and served with 88th Division in Italy; commissioned in 1948; 1952 in Korea commanding 7th Bn 3rd Partisan Infantry Regiment and later in 77th Special Forces Group, 101st Airborne Division; discharged 1960. 1964 saw him in 'Mad Mike' Hoare's mercenaries in Katanga (Congo); 'deported' by CIA. Joined Rhodesian army in 1976 as a captain; in November 1978 he was in America running for Congress in Florida.

101. Panama: National Guardsman, 1969.

The maroon beret and shoulder strap slides, together with the hairstyle, point unmistakably to an airborne unit. Rank badges are somewhat similar to the U.S. system.

102. Brazil: Sergeant, Brazilian Cavalry, 1972.

Like Argentina and Chile, Brazil still employs horsed cavalry in certain parts of the country where the terrain severely limits vehicular movement. Under the stripes can be seen the cavalry badge—crossed lances. Other corps badges are infantry—crossed rifles on a hand grenade; artillery—a grenade; engineers—a tower; armour—head-on view of a tank. Badges of rank for soldiers are similar to the U.S. system and are worn on the upper arm in service and working dress, on the collar in shirt sleeve order. Officers wear five-pointed gold stars on the shoulder, one to three through captain; field officers repeating this scheme but adding a large gold and silver star burst enclosing the green and yellow cockade and five silver stars on a blue ground of the national crest at the base of the shoulder strap.

103. Brazil: Private, Infantry, 1972.

Brazilian army webbing is very similar to the U.S. pattern items but they use the FN N.A.T.O. 7.62 mm. SLR and the Danish Madsen (11.43 mm. as opposed to the Danish 9 mm. model) machine-pistol and called the INA-953 in Brazil. It weighs 3.15 kg. (3.74 with 32 round magazine) is 53 cm. long (78 cm. with folding butt extended), has a 20 cm. barrel, 500-550 rpm rate of fire, effective range 100 m., blow-back operation, muzzle velocity 280 m./sec.

104. Malaya: Soldier, Malayan Races Liberation Army, 1953.
This organization failed in its attempt to subvert Malaya to Communism immediately following World War II. It was mainly Chinese-recruited and this may be a factor pointing towards its lack of popularity with the indigenous population of the state. He carries the U.S. M-1 Carbine, webbing made up of British 1937 pattern items and modified parachute drop harness. At his left hip is a local machete (panga).

105. Cyprus: EOKA Soldier, 'Andarte' Group, 1956.
He carries the Wehrmacht 1944 pattern Sturmgewehr, copied (in concept) from the AK 47. It is a gas operated, 7.9 mm. semi-automatic weapon, 95 cm. long; barrel length 41 cm., weighing 4.62 kg. with 30 round magazine; rate of fire 500 rpm, effective range (bursts) 300 m., muzzle velocity 650 m./sec.

106. Kenya: Mau-Mau General, 1952.
This figure, with home-made rifle and panga is based on personal observation by Mike Chappell. On the shoulders are five red, yellow and green 'pips' indicating rank.

The Mau-Mau preyed mainly on their own tribe—the Kikuyu—who suffered most during the emergency which preceded Kenyan Independence. One of Mau-Mau's leaders (Jomo 'Burning Spear' Kenyatta) later became Kenya's first president.

107. Israel: Paratroop Corporal, Six Day War (5th-10th June), 1967.
Israeli army soldiers' ranks are worn on the upper arms as follows: Turai—Rishon—one bar; Rav-Turai—two; Samal—three; Samal Rishon —three with a superimposed bronze fig leaf. Warrant officers wear bronze badges on the cuff; Rav-Samal—a fig leaf within a six-pointed star all within a laurel wreath; Rav-Samal-Rishon—as above but the central badge is a sword and olive branch instead of a fig leaf. Officers'

ranks are worn on the shoulder in bronze; Mamak (officer cadet)—a silver bar; Segen Mishneh—one bronze bar; Segen—two; Seren—three; Rav-Seren—a fig leaf; Sgan-Aluf—two; Aluf-Mishneh—three; Tat-Aluf—crossed sword and olive branch; Aluf—as before under a fig leaf; Rav-Aluf—as before but two fig leaves. This man carries the Israeli-produced UZI (see figure 251), here with collapsible butt.

108.   Israel: Tank Corps Major, 1967.

Regimental identity is shown by the cap badge (on red backing for combat units): armour—side profile of a tank; artillery—a gun; engineers—a vertical sword behind a tower all on a twelve-pointed star; infantry—a sword and olive branch; signals—a winged vertical sword between lightning flashes; medical—serpent and staff under the star of David; ordnance—sword, flaming grenade and cog wheel; supply—sword, horse-drawn chariot, crossed ears of barley; bands—a lyre; all badges are above a scroll and within a wreath.

109.   Israel: 1st Lieutenant (Segen), Territorial Defence Corps, attached to the NAHAL organization.

The Nahal organization have responsibility for the agricultural settlements hence the sickle and sword arm badge. They also carry out their own first-line self defence. Israeli women soldiers are not employed in combat roles but do undergo arms training.

110.   Egypt: Paratrooper, 1973.

Helmet and AK47 are Russian (see figure 159 for technical details); the camouflage is designed for the desert environment. Badges of rank of soldiers are worn on the upper arms and follow the British scheme except that a five-pointed star is used instead of a crown and the CSM wears an eagle over four white chevrons; a warrant officer wears the Egyptian eagle on both cuffs. Officers wear their five-pointed gold stars on the shoulder, the system is as for the British army—with the eagle replacing the crown—except when dealing with general officers.

111.   Egypt: Major General, 1977.

Service dress is very much as for the British army, but the shoulder boards are green for general officers, the rank badges thereon being crossed sabre and baton, star and eagle in ascending order. Brigadiers have the eagle over sabre and baton; lieutenant general eagle, two stars (side by side) and crossed sabre and baton; general—as before but three stars in triangular formation.

112. Egypt: Infantryman, 1967.
This man carries the Soviet RPD light machine-gun with drum magazine (see plate 160 for technical details) and the Soviet NBC satchel with respirator. In service dress regimental brass badges are worn on the collar (and facing colour is worn as backing to rank badges) as follows: infantry—a charging soldier within a wreath (blue); armour—a winged horse rising out of a tank between two vertical lances (green); artillery —a flaming grenade (black); engineers—three wagon wheels splashing through water (khaki); signals—two lightning flashes over two wings in a wreath (khaki); paratroopers—not known (crimson); medical— serpent and staff within a wreath (khaki); ordnance—a trophy of arms (khaki); supply—an eight-pointed star (khaki); maintenance—a cog wheel within a wreath (khaki).

113 and 114. Lebanon: Christian Militiamen.
Following the Lebanese civil war and the intervention of the Syrian Arab Peacekeeping Force in the struggle, the Christian minority in Lebanon have withdrawn into the west and south of the country and obtain much support from the Israelis. The Christian Militia has recently been in action against the newly reconstituted Lebanese Army and refuse to allow the UNIFIL (U.N. Interim Force in Lebanon) troops access to the areas they control. They are also violently opposed to the PLO who operate in Arab-controlled areas of the country. The weapon is the AK47—see plate 159 for technical details.

115. Lebanon: Muslim Irregular.
In the chaos of modern Lebanon arms from East and West find their way into opposing hands; here the U.S. M-16 carbine (see plate 200 for technical details) is used by the Arab equivalent of the Christian Militia.

116. Saudi Arabia: Lieutenant Colonel, Engineers, 1976.
There is great similarity between the corps badges of the Saudi and the Egyptian army (both worn on the collar); the main difference being that Saudi badges are surmounted by a crown which is replaced by a star and crescent for the Egyptian equivalents. The same applies to rank badges except that soldiers' chevrons are worn point up instead of point down and Saudi's wear a crown instead of the Egyptian eagle.

117. Lebanon: 1st Sergeant, Artillery, 1960.

In March 1975 a vicious civil war, based on religious lines—Christian upper-classes versus Muslims—broke out in the Lebanon. In the following turmoil the Lebanese army dissolved. It has recently been reformed at about battalion strength but is composed almost entirely of Arabs. Soldiers wear chevrons as for the British army with the star replacing the crown; officers also follow the British system with gold, five-pointed stars—one to three through captain, the senior captain wears a star in a wreath and field officers repeat the system but their stars are all over a star in a wreath and all bear a cedar tree in the centre. Brigadiers have crossed sword and baton over the star within a wreath.

Regimental colours are worn on the collar patches; armour—light grey; artillery—red; engineers, signals and logistic troops—black; infantry—blue; medical—crimson; transport—dark green.

The weapon is the U.S. M-3A1 11.43 mm. (.45 inch) General Motors machine-pistol, it weighs 3.71 kg. (4.6 with 30 round magazine; length 57.7 cm. (75.6 with butt extended); 20.3 cm. barrel; rate of fire 350-450 rpm, effective range 90 m.; muzzle velocity 280 m./sec.

118. Iran: Sergeant, Tank Troops, 1979.

Iran bought arms and advice from East and West with its oil riches; Britain supplied Chieftain tanks, America sold anti-tank missiles and the small arms are the G3 as used by West Germany (see plate 253 for technical details). Soldiers' rank badges follow the U.S. army system from Private 1st Class (one chevron) through 1st Class Sergeant (three chevrons over two arcs). Next come the technician specialists— 'Hofomars'—who wear one, two or three gold bars edged black on each shoulder. Officers wear five-pointed gold stars on the shoulder, second lieutenant through captain—one to three respectively; field officers wear larger, eight-pointed silver stars bearing in the centre the lion and sword—major—one; lieutenant colonel—two; colonel—three; general officers wear the imperial crown in gold over the large silver stars thus—brigadier—one crown over the star; major general—the crown over two stars; lieutenant general—the crown over three stars in triangular formation; general—the crown over four stars in a square. Regimental badges are worn in brass on the collar; cavalry—crossed sabres; armour—crossed sabres behind the front profile of a tank; artillery—crossed gun barrels; engineers—a tower within a triangle; signals—crossed lightning flashes; infantry—a flaming grenade;

medical two snakes entwined around a goblet; transport—head-on profile of a lorry; technical—crossed lightning flashes on a cog wheel; bands—a lyre.

119. Syria: Corporal, Infantry, 1973.

The camouflage suit is based on current British army DPM with the green dye removed. Helmet, webbing and AK47 are Soviet supplied (see plate 159 for technical details). While lance corporals and corporals wear their chevrons point down; the senior NCOs wear them point up as follows: sergeant—two; staff sergeant—three; master sergeant—three over a white, five-pointed star; first sergeant—three over two stars. Officers wear gold, five-pointed stars on the shoulder, second-lieutenant through Captain—one to three respectively; major—an eagle; lieutenant colonel—an eagle over a star; colonel—an eagle over two stars side-by-side; brigadier—an eagle over three stars in a triangle; major general—crossed sabres under the eagle; lieutenant general—crossed sabres under two eagles; general—three eagles over crossed sabres. In service dress regimental collar patches (in the facing colour) with brass badges are worn; examples are: armour—light grey with an advancing tank within a wreath; artillery—dark blue with crossed gun barrels within a wreath; infantry—dark green with crossed rifles in a wreath; cavalry (colour unknown)—crossed lances within a wreath; engineers—light brown; signals—dark brown; medical—crimson; military police—red piped black with an upright sword behind a shield and under a scroll.

120. Sultanate of Muscat: Private, Baluch Guards Battalion, 1972.

Many of Oman's soldiers are enlisted from the Pakistani province of Baluchistan; indeed it was only in 1970 that Omani natives were recruited for their country's own armed forces and the Baluch element has now dropped to about 40 per cent. The Sultan of Muscat's forces are armed with British small arms (see plates 221–24 for technical details). Badges of rank are very similar to the British system except that officers wear gold, five-pointed stars and silver Omani crowns.

121. Abu Dhabi: Major, Signals, Defence Force, 1976.

The cap and belt plate badge are the eagle within a circular scroll, the collar badge is the eagle, and on the shoulder appears the shoulder title (ADDF in Arabic script) under the rank badge of the eagle. The arm flash is the signals squadron badge. The brick-red shirt is designed to blend in with the sands of the Liwa area where the army operates. Rank badges follow the British pattern with the eagle replacing the crown.

122.   Iran: Infantryman, 1978.
The U.S. style helmet, uniform and webbing are seen here with the West German G3 7.62 mm. SLR (see plate 253 for technical details). An Iranian brigade fought against Communist-inspired insurgents in the Omani province of Dhofar in 1972-75 and helped to bring that campaign to a successful conclusion.

123.   Oman: Second Lieutenant, Scouts, 1971.
The British army has traditionally supplied many volunteers to serve in the armies of the Gulf States and in fact the Trucial Oman Scouts was raised by the R.A.F. Regiment in 1946 as the Trucial Oman Levies. Rank badges are as in the British army; the cap badge is crossed daggers over a scroll but only officers wear the silver daggers on the shirt collars.

124.   Muscat: Corporal, Sultan's Armed Forces, 1974.
This plate shows desert operations dress with the shmag tied tightly around the head and plimsolls providing light and adequate footwear.

125.   Nepal: Corporal, Devi Dutt Regiment, Parade Dress, 1972.
The yellow hat badge and tourie denote the regiment, the red diamond on the arm is the brigade badge. The system of rank badges is similar to that in the British army and British small arms are used (see plates 221-24 for technical details). For daily wear the Gurkhas wear their famous bush hat, shirt and jersey instead of the Chinese-style tunic seen here.

126.   Nepal: Major, Artillery, Service Dress, 1974.
Prior to 1971 the Nepalese army wore British SD with gold buttons and gold and silver rank badges, but this oriental costume with black buttons and badges, replaced it in that year. Regimental shoulder titles (in Nepali script) are worn under the rank badges; for all combatant officers these commence at the base with crossed kukris and proceed in seniority as follows: 2nd lieutenant—the Kukris alone: 1st Lieutenant— a moon; captain—a sun; major—a sun over a moon; lieutenant colonel —two suns; colonel—two suns over a moon. General officers wear the

kukris within a laurel wreath; brigadier—just the wreathed kukris; major general—a moon over the kukris; lieutenant general—a sun over the kukris; general—a sun over a moon over the kukris.

127. Pakistan: Major General, 1976.
Rank badges are as in the British army except that the crown is replaced by the star and crescent; the Denison smock camouflage pattern (worn by British airborne forces) has been adopted here.

128. Pakistan: Sergeant, Infantry, Battle Order, 1971.
In this year East Pakistan (with much support from India) rose against West Pakistan and seized independence to become Bangladesh. The Pakistani army in East Pakistan lost 60,000 prisoners. The SMG is a later mark of the famous 9 mm. blowback STEN. The gun has here two 32-round magazines taped together to enable quick changes to be made in action without interrupting seriously the firing rate. It weighs 2.99 kg (empty), is 76.2 cm. long with a 19.6 cm. barrel, effective range 75 m., rate of fire 540 rpm, muzzle velocity 400 m./sec.

129. India: Lieutenant, Airborne Artillery, 1971.
The Denison Smock, red beret, 1937 pattern web equipment and Webley and Scott, six-round revolver are all very British as is the cap badge which is identical to that of the Royal Artillery except that the crown is replaced by a five-pointed star. The revolver uses .455 in. cartridges, weighs 1.08 kg. empty, has a 15.2 cm. barrel, effective range 45 m.; muzzle velocity 183 m./sec.

130. India: Indian Signaller, Kashmir, 1965.
The signaller carries the British 'A 41' manpack set with associated satchels and aerial rod case in addition to his own small pack and pistol. Mountains limit communications by radio quite severely.

131. France: Private, 13 Demi-Brigade, Legion Étranger, 1954.
The white kepi cover, epaulettes, aiguillette and waist sash are parade items.

132. France: Colonial Paratrooper, 1952.
The helmet provides a handy place to keep cigarettes and matches; the weapon is the M1 .30 calibre carbine with folding butt. This is a gas operated weapon with 45.7 cm. barrel, 150 m. effective range, 90.4 cm.

153

long with butt extended, rate of fire 30 rpm; muzzle velocity—610 m./
sec., 15-round magazine.

133.　France: Tirailleur Algérien, 1953.
This regiment later formed the basis of Algeria's army. He carries the
MAS-36 rifle. His light blue arm patch has double green edging and
green crescent over a green '7'.

134.　North Vietnam: Viet Cong Guerrilla, 1967.
The Viet Cong in the Vietnam War were supposed to be exclusively
recruited from the South Vietnamese population but particularly after
the Tet offensive of 1968, in which the Viet Cong were practically
destroyed, their ranks were filled with North Vietnamese 'volunteers'.
On the hat is the wearer's name; he carries a black bandolier full of rice,
an AK 47 (see plate 159) together with magazine and grenade pouches.

135.　South Vietnam: ARVN Ranger, 1972.
Another, large scale assault by Viet Cong and North Vietnamese forces
was launched on South Vietnam from Laos and Cambodia in 1972. The
Army of the Republic of Vietnam (ARVN) was by now U.S. trained and
equipped but due to the national emergency (which had lasted from
1958) many of the soldiers involved in the fighting seem to have been
scarcely more than schoolboys. He carries a US M-16 carbine (see
plate 200). Although heavily influenced by their American allies in
many things, the South Vietnamese evolved their own system of rank
badges (after discarding those inherited from the French in 1955).
NCOs (and soldiers) wear a small round silver badge enclosing a vertical
flaming sword; rank badges consist of chevrons worn on the left arm
(point downwards) or (in smaller size) over the left breast pocket in
combat dress. Private 1st Class—one yellow; corporal—two; chief
corporal—one silver over two gold; sergeant—one silver; 1st sergeant
—two; chief sergeant—three silver chevrons. Officers' rank badges
were similar to those worn by the Japanese army and were worn on
black shoulder boards (with a central gold stripe) in service dress; both
collars and on the hat in fatigues and combat dress. Junior officers wore
from one to three gold plum blossoms on plain gold braid; field officers
had silver plum blossoms on embossed gold braid and generals wore
from one to three five-pointed silver stars on embroidered gold lace.
Officers' gold hat badges showed the national eagle with a striped
shield on the chest all on a shield over a scroll (bearing VIÉTNAM

CŌNGHŌA) under a sunburst and flanked by two stylised eagles.

Regimental badges seem not to have been worn although formation patches were worn on the upper left sleeve. Airborne forces wore the maroon beret with silver parachute and gold wings. Rangers wore a hat badge consisting of a yellow shield bearing a black warriors head on a white, five-pointed star.

136.   North Vietnam: Infantry Private, Cambodia [Kampuchia], 1979.

Since the collapse of the South Vietnamese regime in 1976, the North Vietnamese have occupied Laos and Cambodia, destroying in the process the 'Khmer Rouge' regime of the latter country. This drive against the Khmer Rouge led to the Chinese retaliatory invasion of North Vietnam in March 1979 and to the fighting extending to the borders of Thailand by June of the same year. His weapon is the AK 47 of Soviet supply (see plate 159). This army wears red collar patches (in service and working dress) showing rank and regiment in a system very similar to that of the Red Chinese army except that officers wear their silver stars over one bar (for juniors) and two (for field officers). Generals have from one to four gold stars and their collar patches are edged gold.

137.   North Vietnam: Infantry Sergeant, 1979.

As in the Red Chinese army the infantry have no corps badge on their collar patches. Other corps badges (worn to the rear of the silver rank stars) are: armour—a tank in three-quarter profile; artillery—crossed gun barrels; pioneers—crossed pick and shovel over a half cog wheel; signals—a circle with a lightning flash over radio waves; transport—a steering wheel resting on waves; technical services—crossed rifles on a cog wheel; medical—a red cross on a silver, round disc. The fire-power of the Soviet weapons, coupled with over twenty years of constant battle experience, enabled the North Vietnamese to cause the Chinese very heavy casualties in their '79 invasion.

138.   Mongolia: Lieutenant Colonel, Infantry, 1974.

In political terms, Mongolia leans more towards Moscow than Peking at present and the uniform shown here could be mistaken for that of the Soviet army as could the Combat dress. Just after World War II, the Mongolian officers wore a system of symbolic knots on their shoulder boards but these have now been replaced by Soviet pattern stars.

139.   Nationalist China: Military Police Staff Sergeant, 1978.
In contrast to the Red Chinese army, the Taiwanese forces have become very Americanized in general appearance. Corps badges are worn on the collar in this form of dress and on round brass discs for soldiers. The MP's badge (crossed pistols beneath an open book and under a flower blossom) appears on the belt plate and the red, white and blue chest badge, bearing a golden unicorn, is an emblem also peculiar only to the MP's. Badges of rank are worn on the arm (as here) or on the collar in fatigues and are similar to the U.S. army system. Weapons and equipment are American.

140.   U.S. Army in Vietnam: Specialist, 5th Class, 1965.
We see here the summer walking out uniform with regimental collar badges.

141.   U.S. Army in Vietnam: Airborne Trooper, 1970.
Standard U.S. equipment complete with jungle boots; the bottle in the helmet band is probably insect repellant. He wears the famous 101st Airborne's 'Screaming Eagles' formation sign.

142.   U.S. Army in Vietnam: Sergeant, 1st Class, 7th Special Forces Group, 1963.
The 'Green Berets' have a fighting reputation second to none and this N.C.O. has obviously 'been around'. On the shoulder straps are worn small enamelled badges which are traditionally linked to individual battalions of the fighting arms and equate to British regimental cap, collar, and button badges.

Black and White Plate Descriptions

143.   Soviet Personal Equipment.
Top to bottom: Basic 'skeleton order' of brown leather, the left pouch holds magazines for the AK 47; water bottle and entrenching tool are at the rear and grenades are carried in the right pouch. The Soviet respirator is still of the old-fashioned type with a long tube connecting the rubber head mask to the filter unit which remains in the haversack. To the right is the small leather pouch used by men armed with the SKS

rifle. Below left is the round-bottomed pouch for the drum magazines of the RPD MG. The pack is fitted with four strap loops to hold the folded greatcoat or raincape. The Soviet helmet is remarkably similar to the U.S. item in profile.

144/156. Soviet Insignia.

In 1971 new uniforms began to be issued and they included arm badges (worn on the upper left arm) which expressed regimental and corps identity. *Top row:* **144.** armoured troops—black and yellow with red star. **145.** brass collar badge, armoured troops, this badge remained unchanged by the 1971 uniform reforms. **146.** airborne forces—light blue and yellow with red star.

Second row: shoulder boards for field uniform, Khaki with red embellishments. **147.** lance corporal. **148.** senior sergeant. **149.** sergeant major. **150.** lieutenant (one red stripe). **151.** major (two red stripes).

Third row: collar patches. **152.** armoured troops (parade, pre-1970; everyday and parade since then)—gold and black. **153.** artillery (daily wear, pre-1970) gold and black. **154.** motor rifles (field) matt bronze on khaki. **155.** Cyrillic gold letters worn since 1971 on parade and service shoulder boards by junior other ranks; they stand for 'Soviet Army'. **156.** length of service badges for other ranks; worn on the lower left sleeve; they are gold on red and here denote 5 to 9 years' service.

157/160. Soviet Infantry Weapons.

157. APS (*Stetschkin*) 9 mm. pistol with the wooden holster shown here being used as a detachable butt. The weapon weighs 0.76 kg. unloaded; 1.78 kg. with butt. Barrel length 12.6 cm.; weapon length 22 cm. length with butt 54 cm. Effective range—up to 100 m., rate of fire—725 rpm.; the magazine holds 20 rounds. This weapon can fire single shots or bursts and is thus often called a machine-pistol.

Left to right: **158.** SKS (Self Loading Carbine (*Simonow*) 7.62 mm. rifle. This is a World War II vintage weapon no longer used by combat units of the Warsaw Pact Forces but often seen in the Third World. It has been built under licence in China (Type 56), Egypt (Raschid) and Yugoslavia (M-59 and M59/66). Its bayonet is permanently attached and folds down under the barrel. Length 1.022 m. (or 1.25 m. with bayonet fixed), barrel length .52 m.; effective range 400 m. Gas operated with piston; 30 rpm.; 10 shot magazine with the M-43 cartridge. **159.** AK 47 (*Kalaschnikow*). Perhaps the best known and certainly the most numerous infantry carbine in the world. Originally designed and produced during World War II, it has been copied by many states including China (Type 56), Czechoslovakia (M-58), Finland (M/60, M/62), East Germany (MPiKM), North Korea (Type 58, Type 68), Poland (PMK-DGN), Rumania and Hungary. It is a gas operated weapon operating on single shot or burst at 600 rpm.; 7.62 mm. calibre, barrel length .413 m. overall length .87 m. (1.070 with bayonet fixed); 30 shot magazine using the M-43 round; weight 3.8 kg. unloaded; effective range 400 m. Versions with collapsible butts have been produced.

160. RPD (*Roschnoi Pulemet Detjarew*) 7.62 mm. LMG. Once again, a World War II weapon with drum magazine holding a belt of 100 M-43 cartridges. An improved version is the Soviet RPDM and it has been copied in China (Type 56 and Type 56-1) and in Korea (Type 62). Barrel length .52 m.; overall length 1.035 m.; effective range 800 m.; weight with bipods 7.08 kg. (8.8 kg. with full magazine); rate of fire—variable 650-750 rpm.

161/168.   Soviet Headdress.
Top to bottom: **161.** officers' khaki field service cap with khaki plastic cockade. **162.** Khaki side cap for other ranks with red and gold star badge. **163.** Khaki tropical hat with red and gold star. **164.** Winter grey fur cap 'USCHANKA' with red and gold star. **165.** Military police helmet, red and white—often bears cyrillic 'P' (R) for 'Regulators' as traffic police are called. **166.** light blue paratroopers' beret with new style OR's red and gold badge. **167.** Paratroopers' brown leather jump helmet. **168.** Tank crewmen's padded helmet with earphones.

169/172.   Warsaw Pact Headdress.
Top to bottom: **169.** Square-topped Polish army Czapka in olive drab with silver eagle badge—worn in fatigue dress. **170.** Polish mountain troops headdress—Edelweiss brooch to eagle feather plume. **171.** Hungarian field cap with khaki (plastic?) cockade. **172.** Czechoslovakian camouflage field cap with khaki (plastic?) badge bearing a rampant lion.

173.   Yugoslav Mountain Trooper.
The white camouflage and snow goggles are international for these specialist troops; his weapon is the Yugoslav produced M-56 machine-pistol using the 7.62 mm. P (Tokarew) cartridge. Weight 3.06 kg. (3.6 kg. with full magazine of 32 rounds); barrel length .25 m.; overall length .64 m. (.87 m. with butt extended; 1.04 m. with butt extended

and bayonet fixed); effective range 100 m. It is a blow-back weapon with a firing speed of 600 rpm.

174/175. Poland.

Left: **174.** Major, summer camouflaged combat suit with the square-topped czapka and 9 mm. PM (Pistolet Makarowa) Soviet pistol with 8 round magazine; effective range 50 m.; weight .73 kg. (.81 kg. with full magazine); barrel length 9.8 cm., overall length 16 cm. With a muzzle velocity of about 330 m./sec., this is a relatively low-powered weapon. On the shoulder straps are the two silver bars under a star which signifies a major.

Right: **175.** Warsaw Pact, grey rubber NBC suit. The great problem with NBC clothing is the strains it places on the wearer, particularly in hot weather.

176/188. French and Warsaw Pact Insignia.

Top row: **176.** French Arm badge, Foreign Legion (dark green on dark blue). **177.** French corporal's chevrons (red on dark blue). **178.** French major's rank bars on camouflage jacket—brass bars on dark blue. **179.** French regimental device (pocket badge) of the 5th Infantry Regiment of the Foreign Legion (the Legion grenade on the map of Indo-China). *Second row:* **180.** Bulgarian combat dress shoulder boards —junior lieutenant (khaki, red stripe, silver star)—**181.** sergeant major (khaki, red edging and braid). **182.** Polish army woven cap badge. **183.** German Democratic Republic shoulder straps—Stabsgefreiter (corporal)—**184.** Unterfeldwebel (junior sergeant). *Bottom row:* **185.** Hungarian cockade (gold star and surround, red over white over green oval). **186.** Yugoslavian shoulder straps sergeant (two red chevrons)—**187.** junior lieutenant (gold star). **188.** Rumanian mountain troops silver shoulder badge.

189. United States Personal Equipment.

Khaki webbing and blackened metal fittings, widely used in the Middle and Far East. The small pouch on the right brace is for the field dressing; the two front pouches for ammunition and the small pack at the rear holds washing and eating equipment as well as rations. The folding entrenching tool can be worn as convenient around the belt, clipped through the many holes provided.

190/198. United States Army Insignia.

(Rank badges—gold on dark blue)—**190.** Private First Class. **191.** Sergeant Major. **192.** Specialist 5th Class. **193.** Captain's combat badge of rank (matt black on olive drab). **194.** Fatigue dress name tag (worn on right breast)—white with black letters. U.S. Army badges for (**195**) combat and (**196**) fatigue dress (black on olive drab); old pattern (gold on dark blue). Black on olive drab combat and fatigue arm patches. **197.** Airborne and special forces. **198.** 1st Air Cavalry Division.

199/201. United States Infantry Weapons. 199. M60 7.62 mm. light machine-gun. Produced by Bridge Tool & Die Manufacturing Coy Inc. Overall length 1.105 mm., barrel length .65 m., effective range 600 m., gas operated action, 550-600 rpm, belt fed using the N.A.T.O. round giving up to 840 m./sec. muzzle velocity, weight 10.46 kg. Later versions include the M 60E1; the heavy MG version is called the M 122 (with range up to 1,100 m.), the helicopter version is the M 60C and the version produced in Taiwan is termed the M 60D. The IRA have recently been supplied with these weapons from America. **200.** M 16A1 Armalite SLR. Made by Colt, this weapon has a calibre of 5.56 mm., it weighs 2.95 kg. (3.18 kg. with bipod added). There are two magazines—20 or 30 round; rate of fire 700-800 rpm; effective range 300 m.; barrel length .508 m.; overall length .99 m.; muzzle velocity 990 m./sec. **201.** M 14 7.62 mm. Springfield SLR. This gas-operated weapon weighs 3.94 kg. with an overall length of 1.117 m.; barrel length .558 m.; effective range 300 m.; rate of fire 750 rpm; 20 round magazine; muzzle velocity up to 840 m./sec.

202/209. United States Army Headdress.
202. Enlisted man's dark green, peaked garrison cap. **203.** Dark green beret of a captain, Special Forces (crimson patch, silver bars). **204.** Enlisted man's 'overseas cap'. **205.** Steel helmet with plastic liner, steel shell, camouflage cover and circular band for twigs, etc. Fatigue caps (**206**—1950; **207**—1960 style with senior sergeant's matt black rank chevrons). **208.** Winter khaki pile cap. **209.** Vietnam jungle camouflage hat.

210. British 1958 pattern Web Equipment.
Olive drab webbing (requiring no cleaning or blancoing); the bayonet holder behind the pouch does away with a separate bayonet frog; below the two 'kidney pouches' is the cape carrier. The rigid shovel is being replaced by a much smaller folding entrenching tool.

211/220. British Insignia.
211. Royal Artillery Korean War brassard (red letters on dark blue) with light blue Commonwealth Division badge. **212.** Second lieutenant's epaulette slide (black star). **213.** Berlin Field Force arm patch, red on black. **214.** Old pattern sergeant's chevrons (here red on white for wear by certain regiments in tropical khaki drill). **215.** New pattern white on khaki for service dress. **216.** Battle Dress sleeve of a company sergeant major, Parachute Regiment, 1955; lettering and Pegasus light blue on crimson; this man is a despatcher. **217.** Lance corporal, marksman, signaller, 1st Bn Gloucestershire Regiment, 1957, with five years' service, lettering white on red; presidential citation royal blue edged gold (for Imjin River, Korea), yellow, red and blue Wessex brigade diamond patch. **218.** Sleeve of Jungle Green jacket worn by sergeant, 1st Bn Royal Hampshires, 1954. Yellow lettering on black, light blue and white parachute wings, white on dark green Gurkha Brigade patch, white chevrons. **219.** SD sleeve of corporal, Light Infantry, 1960; dark green chevrons on buff. **220.** sleeve of DPM camouflage jacket; black chevrons on khaki.

221/224. British Infantry Small Arms.
221. L-7A2 7.62 mm. FN General Purpose Machine-Gun, Belgian designed N.A.T.O. weapon, 1.255 m. long; barrel length .569 m.; effective range 600 m.; a gas-operated weapon with variable rate of fire 700-1000 rpm; belt fed (500 or 200 round belts) using the N.A.T.O. round with up to 840 m./sec. muzzle velocity. Weight 10.84 kg. with bipod. **222.** L-1A1 FN 7.62 mm. SLR. This gas operated weapon uses the same N.A.T.O. cartridge as the GPMG; length 1.09 m.; barrel length .533 m.; weight 4.32 kg. unloaded; 20 round magazine; effective range 300 m. **223.** 4.85 mm. Individual Weapon (IW). This new weapon (known as Bullpup) is currently (1979) undergoing trials. The layout of the rifle will be familiar to those who remember the experimental British weapon produced in about 1946. It is a gas-operated, magazine-fed gun weighing 4.12 kg. with 20 round magazine (.398 kg.). Barrel length 51.85 cm.; overall length 77 cm.; 4 grooves in the barrel with up to 4.5 kg. trigger pull; muzzle velocity 900 m./sec., 4.42 Joules recoil energy; 700-850 rpm. It is made by the Royal Small Arms Factory, Enfield, Middlesex. The 4 x 4 SUSAT optical sight is a standard fitting. The weapon is all steel except the forestock which is nylon. It can be used on right or left shoulder with equal ease. **224.** L-2A3, 9 mm. Sterling Sub Machine-Gun. This replaced the Sten of World

War II and later fame; a blowback weapon with 19.6 cm. barrel (48 cm. length with butt folded; 71 cm. with butt extended) a bayonet can be fixed. It weighs 2.72 kg. (3.74 kg. with bayonet and 34 round magazine). Effective range 75 m.; rate of fire 550 m./sec. Muzzle velocity up to 360 m./sec.

225/235. British Headdress.

225. Jungle hat (olive drab) also issued in light khaki for desert use. **226.** Gurkha hat (6th Gurkha Rifles); these are always two hats sewn together. **227.** Dark blue beret. 1st Bn Gloucestershire Regiment 1950-1979. This regiment wears a small sphinx within a wreath at the back of its headdress to commemorate the Battle of Alexandria (21 March 1801) when they fought back to back to beat off French attacks. **228.** Beige beret of Special Air Service Regiment with the dark blue patch and woven badge known as the 'Winged Dagger'. (The dagger was intended by its originator to be the 'Sword of Excalibur'.) **229.** Steel helmet with IS visor. **230.** 1970 pattern DPM combat cap. **231.** 1950 pattern olive drab combat cap. Three regimental side hats: **232.** Wessex Brigade—Gloucestershires (note back badge) dark blue and red. **233.** Royal Artillery red and dark blue. **234.** 9th/12th Prince of Wales' Own Royal Lancers, red and yellow. **235.** Parachutist's 'Bowler' jump helmet.

236. British Ammunition Technician in Explosive Ordnance Disposal Suit.

This bulky suit was developed to protect our ammunition technical officers (ATOs) from the blast effects of IRA bombs. It consists of several layers of Kevlar—a fibre originally used in the U.S. Space programme and having excellent ballistic protective properties—with extra glass-reinforced plastic shields to chest and pelvis. The helmet has an extremely heavy visor and a built-in radio communications set. As one ATO said to me 'It enables you to be buried in one piece!'

237. British Body Armour.

The situation in Northern Ireland has spurred development of protective clothing including the items shown here: a new, glass-reinforced plastic helmet (lighter than the steel item but with improved ballistic and shock protection); armoured vest (using Kevlar and having non-slip shoulder pads so that the rifle can be used with accuracy); leg shields of glass-reinforced plastic and various models of shields. The riot baton is a slight refinement on Neanderthal Man's club.

238/248.   Insignia, Various Nations.
Federal Germany—238. Oberfeldwebel, combat suit. **239.** Hauptfeld-webel's fatigue and combat shoulder strap slide. The colour of the cloth loop at the base gives the arm of service (infantry—green, tanks—pink, artillery—red, logistic services—blue, signals—lemon yellow, reconnaissance—deep yellow, engineers—black, NBC—crimson). **240.** Unterleutnant. **241.** Arm patch 1st Luftlande-Division light blue with black and white edge and white badge. The three brigades of the division have different coloured badge edgings as follows: 1st—white, 2nd—red, 3rd—yellow. **Italy—242.** Arm patch parachute brigade—red and yellow; shoulder strap rank badges: **243.** warrant officer—three gold stripes on red. **244.** right major—yellow frame and star. **245.** Arm patch (red and yellow) and yellow rank chevrons of a sergeant major, Folgore Division. **Israel—246.** Corporal's white sleeve chevrons. **247.** staff sergeant's chevrons with bronze olive leaf on the red backing used only by 'teeth arm' (fighting) units. **248.** Lieutenant's bronze bars on red backing.

249/252.   French and Israeli Weapons.
249. French 7.5 mm. M-1949/56 MAS (Manufacture d'Armes de Saint-Étienne). A gas-operated, self-loading rifle, effective range 300 m.; weight 4.24 kg. empty (4.47 kg. loaded with a magazine of ten M-1929 rounds); barrel length .526 m.; overall length 1.102 m.; rate of fire 20 rpm; muzzle velocity approximately 800 m./sec. **250.** French MAT (Manufacture d'Armes de Tulle) 9 mm. Machine-Pistol M-1949. A blowback weapon weighing 3.63 kg. empty (4.23 kg. with 32-round magazine); barrel length 22.8 cm.; overall length 40.6 cm. (66.1 with extended butt); rate of fire 600 rpm; effective range 100 m.; muzzle velocity about 400 m./sec. **251.** Israeli 9 mm. UZI Sub Machine-Gun. A highly successful, Israeli-developed weapon also used by the Federal German army (there called the MP2A1-UZ1); the Belgian, Dutch, Peruvian, Portuguese and Thai forces. Apart from the wooden butt, there is a version with collapsible steel butt. It is a blowback weapon, effective range 100 m.; weight 3.51 kg. empty; barrel length 26 cm.; overall length 63.5 cm. (43.2 cm. with butt collapsed); rate of fire 550 rpm; muzzle velocity 400 m./sec. using Parabellum rounds. There are three magazines with 25, 32 or 40 rounds. **252.** Israeli 5.56 mm. GALIL Assault Rifle. Like the UZ1 this gas-operated rifle with collap-

163

sible butt is produced by Israeli Military Industries. Weight 3.9 kg. (4.6 kg. or 4.9 kg. with 35 or 50 round magazine); barrel length 46 cm.; overall length 98 cm. (74 cm. with butt folded); muzzle velocity 990 m./sec.; effective range 300 m.; rate of fire 650 rpm. The magazines hold 35 or 50 rounds.

253/255. Various Small Arms.
253. West German Gewehr G3A3 7.62 mm. Based on the Spanish CETME (Centro de Estudios Técnicos de Materials Especiales); this blowback rifle uses the standard N.A.T.O. cartridge in a 20-round magazine. It weighs 4.25 kg. (4.7 kg. fully loaded); length 1.02 m.; barrel length 45 cm.; effective range 300 m.; rate of fire 550 rpm; muzzle velocity 840 m./sec. **254.** Czechoslovakian 7.65 mm. M-61 Skorpion machine-pistol. This tiny, blowback weapon weighs 1.31 kg. (unloaded); barrel length 11.4 cm.; overall length 27.1 cm. (52.2 with butt extended); effective range 75 m.; rate of fire 700 rpm; 10 or 20 round magazines are available; the 7.65 mm. short Browning cartridge gives a muzzle velocity of approximately 290 m./sec. **255.** Australian 9 mm. F-1A1 sub machine-gun. This Australian-developed blowback weapon is similar to the British Sterling and is made by the Lithgow Small Arms Factory. Weight 3.26 kg. (4.47 kg. with bayonet and full 34-round magazine); barrel length 20.3 cm.; overall length 71.4 cm. (92.7 cm. with bayonet); effective range 75 m.; rate of fire 600 rpm; muzzle velocity 400 m./sec.

256. West German Personal Equipment. (Kampfaüsrüstung).
Students of World War II will doubtless recognise the old Wehrmacht leather equipment pattern, the principle has been retained although webbing is now used for belt, packs and straps; plastic coated webbing for ammunition pouches and for the zip-closed respirator haversack. The equipment has many metal-to-metal fittings and is noisy for night patrol work.

257. West German Muleteer of the Mountain Division Artillery.
The Italian-designed 105 mm. Pack Howitzer breaks down into four mule loads so that artillery support can be provided in mountainous terrain at times when helicopters (the alternative solution to artillery mobility in these areas) may well be grounded by bad weather. The Germans import mules from Sardinia as they carry these heavy loads better than domestic mules. The Austrian mountain artillery use a mix of mules and native Haflinger ponies (the latter for national prestige

reasons although they cannot carry the loads that a mule can).

258/261. Miscellaneous Headdress.
258. French Foreign Legion junior ranks' képi. **259.** French para-trooper's combat cap. **260.** West German Mountain Troops grey field cap with Edelweiss badge—exactly as for World War II. **261.** Malayan Races Liberation Army khaki cap with red star.

262/264. Asian Communist Equipment.
262. Magazine pouches for AK 47 magazines. **263.** Rice-carrying bandolier. **264.** Grenade pouches. Red China, North Korea and North Vietnam use these items.

265/269. Boots.
265. British DMS (Direct Moulded Sole) boot with the short puttee. **266.** Black U.S. field boot with composition sole. **267.** French canvas and rubber patrol boot. **268.** West German mountain troops boot. **269.** South African brown leather DMS boot—used by several African armies.

270/271. Boots.
270. British olive green canvas and rubber jungle boot. Footwear does not last long in the jungle and this boot was specially designed as a cheap, throw-away item. Commercial hockey boots have also proved their worth in this environment. **271.** Viet Cong Jungle Sandal soled with old rubber tyres. **272.** U.S. Vietnam nylon and leather topped boot with steel-reinforced DMS.